# THE EUR UNION

*Creating the Single Market*

## The Rt Hon The Lord Cockfield PC

Wiley Chancery Law

A Division of John Wiley & Sons

London · New York · Chichester · Brisbane · Toronto · Singapore

Published in the United Kingdom by
Chancery Law Publishing Ltd
Baffins Lane
Chichester PO19 1UD

Published in North America by
John Wiley & Sons Inc
7222 Commerce Center Drive
Colorado Springs CO 80919
USA

Typeset by Dorwyn Ltd, Rowlands Castle, Hants

Printed in Great Britain by
Biddles Ltd, Guildford and King's Lynn

ISBN 0-471-952 079

A copy of the CIP entry for this book
is available from the British Library

To my late wife Monica

# Contents

# Introduction

This is not a political memoire. It is the story of the genesis of the most important development in the Community since it was founded, namely the successful completion of the Single Market. I was described by Jacques Delors in the message he wrote in the copy he sent me of his book "*Le Nouveau Concert European*" as "the splendid architect of the single market". This brief tribute encapsulates better than anything else the relationship between us. The Single Market remains the most important achievement of the ten years in which Jacques Delors has been President of the Commission. History will be much kinder to him than his contempories have been. Like many political leaders he stayed on too long: and his reputation has suffered. But in the years we worked together he was at the peak of his powers.

On 17 December 1992 Jacques Delors took the Chair at a Séance Académique in Brussels to celebrate the completion of the Single Market Programme. The speech I made on that occasion is reproduced as an Appendix to this book. It was a brief account of the genesis and the progress of the project. But as history so often is written by people who were not there, did not themselves know what went on, who relied upon accounts given by others, often themselves second or third hand, and not infrequently relied upon their imagination to fill the gap or to tailor history to suit their own conveniences, it is important that as the main player in this drama I should set down exactly what did happen. Not least because the records, always incomplete, are already disappearing.

It is not possible to do this without tracing, however briefly, the history of the Community itself and of the UK's relations with it. It is almost impossible for anyone on the Continent to understand how the British mind works. A thousand years of separate development cannot be cast away in a single day. The customary accusations of hypocracy and perfidy are based on this incomplete understanding – extending at times to a total misunderstanding. Too often there has been no meeting of the minds. Possibly what I have to say will dissipate at least some of that fog.

But first more mundane matters. In the legal documents the Single Market is referred to as the "Internal Market" – that is trade within the Community as opposed to the "External Market" that is trade with countries outside the Community. But with a not unnatural desire to place our own stamp on the project we ourselves have insisted on calling it the "Single Market".

The French with their greater sense of theatre call it the "Grand Marché", or the Great Market, a much more evocative term. In the same way we refer to the "Single European Act" while the French more elegantly call it the "*Acte Unique*". To complicate matters further the programme was commonly referred to simply as "1992" corresponding to the date of 31 December 1992 fixed for the completion of the programme. The terms are interchangeable and I use all three: they all mean the same.

"The Internal Market Programme" as it was described originally was set out in a "White Paper". The term "White Paper" is quintessentially English and at that time was unknown on the Continent. Nothing could illustrate this better than the fact that the true original edition sent to the Heads of Government had red covers. But today even on the Continent the term is coming into more general usage to describe a document setting out matters of grand policy. Thus the recent Commission Document on "Growth, Competitiveness and Employment" for which the Copenhagen European Council asked is called a "White Paper". Much of the White Paper on the Internal Market I wrote myself by hand and indeed I had started drafting before I even came to Brussels. Having been written originally in English the White Paper is an eminently readable document. Had it been written in some third language, translated into French – the working language of the Community – and then retranslated into English, it could well have lost much of its original directness and readability. What can happen to mere words is well illustrated by the fact that "White Paper" has been translated into French as "*Livre Blanc*" and then retranslated into English as "White Book".

While I am concerned primarily to explain the events of the years 1985 to 1988, and in particular the conflicts which arose with the British Government, conflicts which unfortunately still continue, it is essential if these matters are to be understood to know something not only of the background which led up to the production of the White Paper and of the Internal Market Programme but also, as I have indicated, of the early history of the Community and of its development; and above all of the circumstances of our own accession to the Community and of our disputes with our fellow Member States.

The Single Market Programme was no only important in itself but also in pointing the way forward – as the "Signpost to the Future". As I said at the time the Single

Market was not the end of the road but the road that led somewhere: that after the Single Market would come the Single Currency: and after the Single Currency would come the Single Economy. So in due time we will need to look where the Single Market has led – to Maastricht and what lies beyond that and what part we can play in that evolving process. This book deals with the past and the present: the future is still to come.

As a matter of historical interest, two Addresses I delivered after leaving the Commission are included in this book as Appendices. The first is an Address I gave to the European University Institute in Florence in October 1989 which illustrates the way my own thoughts were developing at that time. It was published by the Commission as a contribution to the debate on the future of Europe at a time when the dramatic changes leading to the dissolution of the Soviet Empire and the freeing of the countries of Central and Eastern Europe had barely begun. The second, as I have already said, is the Address I gave to the Séance Académique in Brussels on 17 December 1992, originally intended as a celebration of 1992, which gives a brief account of the evolution of the 1992 Programme.

*19 April 1994*
*The Rt Hon The Lord Cockfield PC*

## Chapter 1
# The Birth of the Community: Britain the Reluctant Bride

## Early history and philosophy

It is often argued that St Paul, who joined the Christian faith some time after the Twelve Apostles, radically altered its direction. Unfortunately, despite trying very hard, the United Kingdom has no chance of doing the same with the European Community.

Commonly the Community is regarded as founded in 1957 by the Treaty of Rome. In fact this is not so. The Community really dates from 1952 with the Coal and Steel Community founded by the Treaty of Paris. At first sight the identification of the Coal and Steel Community as the foundation of the European Community looks very odd. But in fact the connection is a very logical one.

The European Community was the response to the two Great Wars which devastated Europe in the first half of the present century: and it was to the preservation of peace that the Community was directed. This comes out very clearly in the Preamble to the Treaty of Paris:

"CONSIDERING that world peace can be safeguarded only by creative efforts commensurate with the dangers that threaten it", and therefore:

> "RESOLVED to substitute for age old rivalries the merging of their essential interests; to create by establishing an economic community, the basis for a broader and deeper community among peoples long divided by bloody conflicts; and to lay the foundations for institutions which will give direction to a destiny henceforth shared."

The philosophy underlying all this was that wars were the fruit of economic rivalry: and that the way to prevent war was to substitute economic co-operation for economic rivalry. This was to be achieved by the creation of an Economic Community: and because coal and steel were regarded as the sinews of war, it was with "Coal and Steel" that a start was made in the move from societies accustomed to war to a Community committed to peace.

There was another interesting aspect of this. Emile Noel, who had been Secretary General of the Commission since the beginning, told me that Monnet, who was the philosophical inspiration of the Community and who had been Deputy Director General of the old League of Nations, realised that peace in Europe required a rapprochment between Germany and its victorious enemies, France and Britain: but at the same time he realised that so soon after the war the Allies would simply not accept the return of Germany to the fold. So he approached the problem indirectly. Germany was potentially the predominant coal and steel producer in Western Europe: so if one started with coal and steel one had to have Germany in: and this could be presented on technical and not political grounds.

The Coal and Steel Community was followed with barely a pause for breath by the European Defence Community but tragically this was rejected in 1954 by the French

National Assembly. Indeed it was this rejection which led to the founding of the Western European Union (WEU). But undaunted by the rejection of the Defence Community the Founding Fathers pressed ahead and in 1957 the Treaty of Rome was signed establishing the European Economic Community and at the same time a second Treaty of Rome establishing the European Atomic Energy Community. Indeed Emile Noel recounted that it was originally intended that the Atomic Energy Treaty should come first as the natural and logical successor to Coal and Steel but when that ran into difficulties the Founding Fathers decided to take a great leap forward and establish the "Economic Community" which was the ultimate goal laid down in the Treaty of Paris. So they turned their attention to a Treaty to establish a European Economic Community. This Treaty was successfully negotiated and signed in Rome on 25 March 1957. The blockage having thus been cleared the Treaty establishing the Atomic Energy Community was signed simultaneously. So one of the greatest achievements in European history flowed from initial failure elsewhere, a lesson we need to bear in mind when we come to consider the Maastricht Treaty and what lies beyond. In 1967 the three Communities so established were effectively merged to form what is called the "European Community" and this remains the position despite the creation of the "European Union" by the Maastricht Treaty.

From the very beginning the concept was indeed the creation of a European Union– an "ever closer union among the peoples of Europe" as the Treaty of Paris said in the very first line. Interestingly it was to be a union among the "*peoples*"; not between the *states*. The de Gaulle/Thatcher line, seemingly now adopted by the Major Government, of a grouping of sovereign independent states is a latter day heresy devoid of legal or philosophical foundation. But the Treaties did not define what "European Union" meant or was to consist of: that was to come later – first with the Solemn Declaration signed at Stuttgart in 1983, then with the Single European Act and now, with some hesitation, in the Maastricht Treaty.

When the original Treaty of Paris was negotiated the Labour Government of the day had nationalised both coal and steel. As a result they decided to stand aside from the Coal and Steel Community: and when the Conference was convened at Messina in 1955 to deliberate on further steps forward to the "ever closer union" the Conservative Government which had now come into office refused to participate and limited itself to sending a silent observer. Our view was that nothing would come of it: and we dismissed it as mere vapouring by Continentals addicted to rhetoric and not action. We argued that what was needed was simply a free trade area, a concept the British Government still espouse despite the developments of the last 40 years. Perversely the European powers did not share our perception and they went forward with their Community. How right we were and how wrong they were is shown by the fact that when the Community was founded we had the highest *per capita* income in Western Europe: today we are poorer than any of the original members of the Community.

There were political overtones as well. For hundreds of years, and certainly since the time of the Tudors, British foreign policy has been based on the concept of "the balance of power". If the French got too powerful we sided with the Germans: if the Germans got too powerful we sided with the French. The emergence of a Franco-German axis dominating a European Community would destroy the very basis of our traditional foreign policy and undermine our international and political power. One can see precisely the same philosophy at work today: except that we try to apply the "balance of power" approach inside the Community instead of from the outside.

## Britain changes its mind and is belatedly accepted as a member

When the European powers rejected the advice we freely but unwanted offered them and went ahead with their Community, we retaliated by founding the European Free Trade Association or EFTA as it is commonly known. But having established EFTA, and with Harold Macmillan as Prime Minister we almost immediately changed our mind and applied for Community membership. In January 1963 we were indignantly rejected by General de Gaulle who – probably rightly – distrusted our motives and felt that our outlook and attitudes were inimical to Community membership. It is interesting in the light of subsequent events that the Cabinet minutes for that year recently released reveal how alarmed Harold Macmillan was at the prospect of serious public reaction against the surrender of national sovereignty Community membership would entail. There has been a long running and extremely unfortunate sequel in that governments not only then but ever since stand accused of having told the truth but never quite the whole truth. And that is what underlies so much of the bitterness in the battles over the Maastricht Treaty. But unabashed by our rejection we applied again. Harold Wilson was now Prime Minister but we fared no better. In November 1967 we were rejected for the second time. Underlying General de Gaulle's entrenched opposition was the so-called "Special Relationship" between the United Kingdom and the United States with the General deeply suspicious of the United Kingdom as a Trojan Horse for American domination of Europe. Interestingly, this suspicion of Britain as the "Trojan Horse" persists to this day. But in 1967 the General's objections went even deeper. It is interesting to quote two passages from his press conference on 27 November 1967:

> "The Common Market", he declared, "is incompatible with Britain's economy as it stands, in which the chronic balance of payments deficit is proof of its permanent imbalance and which, as concerns production, sources of supply, credit practices and working conditions, involves factors which that country could not alter without modifying its own nature . . .",

and he went on to proclaim that Britain's accession would:

> "mean breaking up a Community that was built and operates according to rules which do not tolerate such a monumental exception."

It is remarkable that more than 25 years on, our "incompatability" with the Community, or more accurately with the other members of the Community, rests on much the same factors, the weakness of our economy which persists despite the recent tentative recovery, our highly individualistic views on economic and monetary policy as well as on industrial and social policy. The detail may have changed but the substance remains. We are now, as then, the "monumental exception". It is significant that Mrs Thatcher who was our own Prime Minister during my term of office in the Commission should have been so strong an admirer of de Gaulle and his approach to the Community. The explanation may well be a Freudian one. She disliked the Community: at heart wished we had never joined; and subconsciously shared the General's analysis of our characteristics which delineated us as the "monumental exception", overlooking the fact that in his eyes it was condemnation while in hers it was praise.

Nevertheless, in 1973 with the departure of the General from the political scene, and with Edward Heath as Prime Minister we were finally accepted as members of the Community. We were joined by Denmark and Ireland and later by Greece, Spain and Portugal. Of the countries remaining behind in EFTA, Austria, Finland, Sweden and Norway have now successfully completed negotiations to join the Community. Interestingly, we are now poorer than any of the present members of EFTA as well as poorer than any of the original members of the Community. So outside of the Community or inside we have made no great success of our economic affairs. Truly "Man does not live by bread alone"; but he has a pretty poor time without it. And I wonder at times whether our indifferent economic success, our mounting problems and our decline in relative prosperity are really adequate compensation for the retention of a sturdy independence in an increasingly interdependent world.

So by the time we joined in 1973, the Community was already 21 years old. It had reached a state of maturity. It had developed a wide range of policies. It was well on the road to Economic Union: and Political Union was then thought to be not far below the horizon. Under the terms of the Treaty of Accession we were bound to accept the "Community acquis", that is the corpus of Community law and policy already established. Traditionally Community policies once accepted are never pulled up and the roots re-examined. They may be adapted or developed to meet changing circumstances: but they are not simply abandoned because someone does not like them. The

Community always goes forward: never backward. At times progress may slow to the point that it appears almost to have stopped: but in due time progress will be resumed. If what has happened in recent years is anything to go by, people in this country – with distinguished exceptions – simply did not understand this. They thought they had a *tabula rasa* on which they could write anything that took their fancy. They did not: and they could not.

It is interesting that this misconception still exists. When in 1992 the then Chancellor of the Exchequer (Lamont) accepted a binding minimum rate of VAT it was greeted in the British Press with screaming headlines accusing him of surrendering British Sovereignty.

"Britain forfeits sovereignty to Brussels on VAT"

proclaimed – the historically correct phrase is probably "trumpeted" – *The Times* on its front page on 28 July 1992. The truth of the matter is that Article 99 of the Treaty of Rome provided for the harmonization of indirect taxation and in turn the VAT was entrenched as the turnover tax of the Community in 1967. Both therefore were part of the Community *acquis* which we were bound to observe under the Treaty of Accession. The demand by the anti-European factions in the media and elsewhere that we should have none of this is a demand that we welch on our Treaty obligations.

## Britain in the Community

Having taken us into the Community, within a few months in February 1974 Mr Edward Heath lost the General Election and was succeeded by a Labour Government under Mr (as he then was) Harold Wilson. Mr Heath was never a man to take kindly to advice and his original decision in January 1974 not to call an election was right: his acceptance of advice a few weeks later to call an election was wrong. It was probably the first time in his life he ever accepted advice: it was a disaster for him: a disaster for his party and a disaster for the country.

The Labour Party was committed to withdrawal from the Community. Instead, once in government, Mr Wilson decided to "renegotiate" the terms of entry. The changes he secured were minimal but sufficient for him to claim that he had succeeded where Mr Heath had failed and that on the revised terms the Community was acceptable to Britain. This verdict, a superb example of political "facing both ways", was confirmed by a massive majority in a Referendum held in 1975.

The quarrels with Britain quenched the last spark of progress in the Community, or so it appeared at the time. And this indeed was probably a major factor in making the Community appear acceptable both to the Labour Party and the anti-European elements which were gaining if not ascendancy at least a powerful position in the Conservative Party.

In May 1979 Mrs Margaret Thatcher, who had ousted Mr Heath as leader of the Conservative Party, won the General Election and became Prime Minister with a substantial majority. I myself became a member of her government as Minister of State at the Treasury and subsequently as a member of her Cabinet first as Secretary of State for Trade and then Chancellor of the Duchy of Lancaster.

Mrs Thatcher's immediate concern in 1979 in inheriting a Britain on the verge of bankruptcy was to staunch the unrequited flow of money to the European Community. In her own words she "demanded her money back''. Of course when we joined the Community in 1973 it was obvious that we would be large net contributors. Indeed General de Gaulle, whom Mrs Thatcher subsequently came to admire because of his vigorous defence of national sovereignty, had succeeded in restructuring the Community finances in such a way as to ensure that if we did become members it would be on terms that we dearly paid for the privilege. The reason why we accepted what was to emerge as a very one sided deal lay in the circumstances described below. The ''marriage contract'' of the Community, to quote Jacques Delors' phrase, was the agreement between France and Germany that France would give German industry free access to its domestic market in return for Germany financing French agriculture. As a result, Germany became the largest net contributor to the Community budget but it equally became the dominant industrial power in the Community. It was in the event a cheap price for Germany to pay. We thought that events would turn out the same way for us: that British industry offered the opportunity of an open market in Europe would greatly prosper and this would more than outweigh the burden of our budgetary contribution.

But events did not turn out that way at all. The Labour Government dominated by the trade unions presided over the decline of British industry and the destruction of its competitiveness: the Thatcher Government halted the decline in competitiveness but was unable to revive the fortunes of manufacturing industry. So we ended up by paying an inflated contribution in return for domination of our domestic markets by German, French and Italian industry.

In the accession negotiations agreement was reached that if an ''unacceptable'' situation arose, corrective action would be taken. The agreement was at official level only but it gave backing for the demands Mrs Thatcher now made. The deal finally secured, first provisionally then more enduringly at the Fontainebleau Summit (in June 1984), took the form of a two-thirds refund of our net contributions (that is, broadly, the amount we paid less the amount we received under the Common Agricultural Policy or by way of regional and other grants). The provisional agreement had been negotiated by Sir Geoffrey Howe as Chancellor of the Exchequer and was regarded as unacceptable by the Prime Minister. I was asked to advise. The view I expressed was that in a difficult negotiation where the cards were stacked against you "splitting the difference", in this instance a 50% rebate, would be an acceptable but not enthusiastic outcome: a 66% rebate *i.e.* two to one, which is what had been negotiated, was a considerable achievement which ought to be accepted before the other side had second thoughts. My advice was accepted but I was told afterwards that it had not been received with good grace. In the event the arithmetic turned out better than had been anticipated: thus, while our net contribution in 1979–80, before the deal was struck was £839 million, in 1980–81 it fell to £168 million and in 1981–82 even further to £117 million (Hansard 18 October 1993 col 13: Written Answers). Although subsequently our net contribution began to rise again, nevertheless when the rebate formula was confirmed on a long term basis at the Fontainebleau Summit in June 1984 it seemed to have brought to an end the unhappy chapter of our early relations with the other members of the Community. It is interesting that the final settlement owed a great deal to President Mitterrand. France had been the foremost opponent of the United Kingdom on this issue. But at Fontainebleau France held the Presidency and Mitterrand felt that it was more important for the French

Presidency to be a resounding success than to win his battle with the United Kingdom on this particular point. The stage was now set fair.

# Chapter 2
# The Forging of the Internal Market Programme

## Preliminary skirmishes

The Fontainebleau Summit in June 1984 solved, or so it was then thought, all the outstanding problems of the Community – the Common Agricultural Policy, budget discipline, own resources and the British budget contribution. There is something depressingly familiar about this litany and it was not to be very long before these matters were to return to haunt us. But for the moment all was sweetness and light. A window of opportunity had opened and it was in these circumstances and in this atmosphere that I agreed to go to Brussels as the Senior UK Commissioner and a Vice President of the Commission.

I had inevitably some connection with the European issue in the 1950s and the 1960s when I was in industry and a member of the Grand Council of the CBI and a founder member of the original National Economic Development Council better known as "Neddy". But my close connection came in the years after 1964 when the Conservative Party was in opposition and I was working with Ted Heath and Iain Macleod on restructuring the fiscal and economic policy of the Conservative Party. This was the period when the Community was first moving into the field of tax harmonization. The Directive prescribing the VAT as the common and only turnover tax or sales tax in the Community was adopted on 11 April 1967. We at that time had two such taxes, the Purchase Tax levied on goods at the manufacturing or wholesale level and the Selective Employment Tax designed essentially to be a tax on services, and notably on wholesale and retail distribution. Neither tax was compatible with the regime now adopted in the Community. It was vitally important therefore to know whether I should be drawing up our plans on the basis that we would be members of the Community or whether we would still be excluded, in which event we could go our own way. When I put this point to Ted Heath he was quite categorical in his reply – we must plan on the basis that we would be members of the Community. The die was now cast and when we won the 1970 Election we were committed to the introduction of the VAT and indeed a vast amount of preparatory work had already been done. Interestingly, Harold Wilson who was then Prime Minister had withdrawn the co-operation traditionally extended to the Opposition six months before the election to enable them to plan the details of their policy against the day that they might come into government: as a result the Customs felt unable to deal with me direct and we had to bring in Professor Wheatcroft as an intermediary. Despite the difficulties this created, by the time we came into office we were ready to move. Tragically, Iain Macleod died only a few weeks after he became Chancellor of the Exchequer and the task of introducing the VAT fell to his successor, Tony Barber. Our European objective was also responsible for our adoption of the imputation system for the corporation tax instead of the more straightforward split rate system. This in turn was the product of inadequate or misleading information. Although our original choice was in favour of a clear split rate system, we were informed at the last minute that Germany was preparing to abandon its split rate system and adopt the French imputation system. The information provided was wrong. The Germans have in fact retained the split rate system as far as the company itself is concerned, combined with an imputation system for the domestic shareholders. But on the basis of the information we had received we decided to change over to the French system and we are thus left with a system which is thoroughly unsatisfactory.

No sooner had we joined the Community than the Conservative Party lost the General Election in February 1974. I had by then become Chairman of the Price Commission and thus removed from active politics. And Mr Heath was replaced by Mr Wilson. Neither of us therefore played any part in the wasted five years – wasted in terms of our Community membership – during the period 1974 to 1979. But in 1979 the Conservative Party won the election under the leadership of Mrs Thatcher. Mr Heath remained rejected but I – by now a member of the House of Lords – entered the government as Minister of State at the Treasury. In 1982 I became Secretary of State for Trade and a member of the Cabinet: and in 1983 Chancellor of the Duchy of Lancaster.

As Secretary of State for Trade I was responsible at Cabinet level for a wide range of Community matters and in particular many of the matters now covered by the term "The Internal Market". The term "The Internal Market" does not appear anywhere in the Treaties and it was not until the Single European Act was signed in February 1986 that it was given legal recognition. The original treaty – the Treaty of Rome – firmly vested *external* trade matters in the Community. But when you looked not at this "external market" but at the "internal market" what you found was not a single corpus of law but an enormous complex of provisions dealing with specific matters of Community competence relating to internal trade in the Community. Pre-eminent among these provisions were those relating to what was described as the "common market" which was to be based upon a "customs union". A customs union is very different from a simple free trade area. It involves a very significant surrender of national sovereignty. Thus, there has to be a common external tariff and a common external trade policy. But the immense advantage of a customs union is that once goods have lawfully entered the territory of the customs union and have paid whatever duties are exigible they are entitled to freedom of circulation throughout the territory of the customs union. There is no need for rules of origin, for certificates of origin or border controls to enforce these rules. Under a customs union tariffs between Member States in the Community would therefore disappear and so too should customs formalities and border controls. Under the terms of the Treaty all this was to be achieved over three periods of four years each *i.e.* a total of 12 years. In fact the Customs Union was completed in 10½ years (in 1967), well ahead of schedule.

It was thought that with the completion of the Customs Union, the frontier controls and ultimately the frontiers themselves would disappear and that we would be well set to achieve the "four freedoms", as they now tend to be called, enshrined in the Treaty of Rome, namely the freedom of movement of goods, persons, services and capital. The Treaty of course included specific measures dealing with all of these subjects, many of them requiring subordinate legislation by way of Regulations, Directives or Decisions: but it was not thought that that would impose any particular difficulties. Unfortunately the reality proved to be very different. Once the tariff barriers were removed it became evident that the non-tariff barriers remained as a very formidable obstacle. Moreover despite the very categorical provisions of the Treaty, little or no progress had been made in important areas such as the services, transport and fiscal harmonization. Nevertheless, with the completion of the Customs Union, the Commission buckled to with a will. Unfortunately events conspired against them. The so called Luxembourg Compromise – agreed in 1966 to placate General de Gaulle who had adopted "an empty chair" policy to frustrate progress in the Community – under which the Member States agreed not to take decisions by majority voting where a Member State felt that its 'very important interests" were at stake, created insuperable difficulties allowing a single Member State effectively to block progress despite what the Treaty said. The enlargement of the Community with Denmark as well as the United Kingdom hostile if not to the Community as such but certainly to any significant move forward, together with the onset of the two oil price-induced recessions in the 1970, brought the Community virtually to a halt.

But in the early 1980s as the Community and the world as a whole emerged from the recession, the flame was rekindled and those who regarded themselves – or were subsequently categorised or criticised – as "Europeans" began to press for completion of the original objectives of the Treaty of Rome. The phrase "relaunching the Community" came into popular use. The European Parliament, directly elected for the first time in 1979, saw the revival of the Community and of the concept of a "European Union" as the key to their own future. But the first task for the Community was to complete the unfinished agenda of the Treaty of Rome. In 1982 a decision was taken to devote a special session of ECOFIN – the Council of Economic and Finance Ministers – to Internal Market matters. What was described as a "Jumbo Council" bringing together Ministers in the various Departments interested in the Internal Market was convened in November 1982 and this in turn led to a decision in January 1983 to set up a new Council, the Internal Market Council, which held its first meeting in February of that year. At that time I was Secretary of State for Trade and many if not most of the subjects dealt with by the Internal Market Council fell within my field of responsibility.

Although the Treaty refers to "the Council", the Council had become a hydra headed monster, new "Councils" continually being created to deal with individual subjects. The Maastricht Treaty has continued this process and the count now approaches 30. The creation of a separate "Council" tends to indicate that the subject matter is regarded as being of particular importance, justifying a specialised "Council" of its own bringing together the appropriate Ministers in the individual Member States.

The establishment of the new Internal Market Council created little stir, perhaps even less in the United Kingdom than elsewhere. Indeed the Department of Trade itself while mildly in favour felt it a bit of a diversion. I myself attended only one of the actual meetings of the Council and even this was an improvement on tradition which dictated that attendance at Council meetings was the task of one of the Ministers of State, the Secretary of State himself dealing only with the issues of policy involved. Nor did the new Council make much of an impression elsewhere nor was its remit – the Completion of the Internal Market – regarded as a very high priority. This comes out very clearly if one looks at the Solemn Declaration on European Union signed at Stuttgart on 19 June 1983 by the Heads of Government and the Foreign Secretaries of the Member States – including in our own case Mrs Thatcher and Sir Geoffrey Howe respectively. If any specific event can be regarded as "relaunching the Community" it was undoubtedly the Solemn Declaration.

The Solemn Declaration not only firmly committed the Community to European Union as its ultimate objective but set out the policies which were to lead it there; and not the least of these policies were Economic and Monetary Union, Social Policy and Economic and Social Cohesion. Interestingly, the Completion of the Internal Market – the "1992" Programme or the "Single Market" Programme as it is now commonly called – came well down the list. It only appears on page 14 of the English translation: and in the title dealing with the "Development of Community Policies" it comes only after a long list of other policies – Economic Strategy: the EMS: Economic and Monetary Union: Economic Cohesion: External Relations: and the Developing Countries. The text refers only to the "remaining obstacles" as though much progress had been made and the obstacles remaining were few in number: and it specifies only the free movement of goods, capital and services, with no reference to "individuals" who seem to have been overlooked.

This somethat cavalier treatment of the Internal Market in the Solemn Declaration is perhaps surprising in view of the fact that the new Internal Market Council had already had its first meeting – in February of the same year. Even stranger, the European Council which met at Fontainebleau in June 1984, and was a crucially important Council, did not refer to the Internal Market at all, although it did concern itself with the "Citizens Europe" and thus to some extent repaired the gap left by the

Solemn Declaration in relation to the freedom of movement of individuals. What then, in the face of this indifference, was it that propelled the Completion of the Internal Market from the humble position it occupied in the Solemn Declaration and its virtual disappearance from the agenda at Fontainebleau to the position of preeminence it was soon to occupy? I personally – perhaps with some pride of parentage – regard the 1992 Programme as the turning point in the Community's history, the foundation on which all future progress has come to rest. It is this dramatic change in emphasis, this "coming in from the cold" that I now set out to explain.

In September 1984 when I was still in the Cabinet as Chancellor of the Duchy of Lancaster I was invited to go to the Commission in Brussels as the UK's Senior Commissioner and Vice President. This was in the immediate aftermath of the Fontainebleau Summit and in what appeared to be the new spirit of co-operation between the United Kingdom and the European Community it seemed that at long last we had the opportunity of making a positive contribution to the development of the Community. Nowhere were the possibilities more obvious than in the task of completing the Internal Market. We in the United Kingdom had a particular interest in this because while good progress had been made in establishing the freedom of movement of goods, in the case of services, and especially financial services where our main interest lay, progress had been poor. This was partly because one can see a lorry carrying goods stopped at the frontier: but you cannot see a banking service or insurance stopped at the frontier. But perhaps just as importantly because France, Germany and indeed other countries simply did not have the interest in liberalising services that the British have: indeed on the contrary many of these countries had a very illiberal approach and wanted to preserve it. The appointment of a British Commissioner to this portfolio might therefore produce a significant change in emphasis.

I discussed the matter with Christopher (Lord) Soames who had been the UK's very first Commissioner when we joined the Community way back in 1973. His knowledge and understanding of the Community was phenomenal. His advice was absolutely clear: I must go for the Internal Market portfolio; otherwise it was not worth my while going to Brussels. I was greatly surprised subsequently to learn that Nigel Lawson, who as Chancellor of the Exchequer was greatly concerned about the burden of the UK budget contribution, had pressed strongly that I should take over the Budget portfolio which had been held by the retiring British Commissioner, Christopher Tugendhat; and that when he was in Washington he had secured the support of Willy de Clercq, the Belgian Finance Minister who had also been nominated as a member of the new Commission and in return he would support Willy de Clercq's ambition to secure the Economic and Monetary Affairs portfolio. I put it to the Prime Minister that if I took the Budget portfolio – which I was not prepared to do – it would reproduce the familiar situation in which the United Kingdom was isolated as a minority of one; while if the Budget went to a reasonably tough neutral (in the event it went to Henning Christophersen, the Dane) there would be at least three of us, namely myself, the Budget Commissioner and Jacques Delors, himself a former Finance Minister with an outstanding reputation for financial prudence, all supporting firm budgetary policy. While therefore there was a strong case *against* my taking the Budget portfolio, there was an even stronger case *for* my taking the Internal Market portfolio where the United Kingdom had a clear interest in ensuring success.

Although legally the allocation of portfolios is a matter for common agreement among the Commissioners themselves, Jacques Delors was determined to get the whole matter cut and dried before the new Commission took office and so to avoid finding himself confronted by the acriminious negotiations and the "night of the long knives" which had bedevilled the early days of former Commissions.

Thus, the stage was set for the discussion which ensued when Jacques Delors came to dine with the Prime Minister and myself at No 10 Downing Street in October 1984. The Prime Minister set out clearly and decisively the case for my taking the Internal Market portfolio and I strongly supported her. Somewhat surprisingly Jacques Delors was not inclined to argue. It needs to be remembered that at that time Mrs Thatcher was the most formidable Head of Government in Europe and her reputation and influence was at its height. Jacques Delors' day was still to come. But I suspect there was another factor at work. Jacques Delors' primary interest had always lain in Economic and Monetary Union and indeed has remained so and I sensed that he was relieved to have the senior British Commissioner safely settled in a portfolio which appealed to the UK Government and would he hoped greatly reduce the prospect of the United Kingdom finding fresh fields of dispute with the rest of the Community. In short what he feared might prove to be a difficult hurdle had been surmounted with apparent ease. Nigel Lawson was clearly disappointed, if not actually disapproving. So far as Willy de Clercq was concerned his ambition came to nothing. Jacques Delors insisted on taking the Economic and Monetary Affairs portfolio himself, although with the assistance of the second German Commissioner, the wise and intensely courteous Alois Pfeiffer, who tragically died in harness.

So perhaps unwittingly but in a very real sense, the Downing Street dinner laid down the foundation of what was in time to emerge as an alliance between Jacques Delors and myself which in turn was to ensure the success of the Single Market Programme.

# Chapter 3
# The Forging of the Internal Market Programme

## The early days and Royaumont

The distribution of portfolios among the members of the new Commission proceeded on the basis Jacques Delors had planned. In addition to the discussion at dinner at No 10, I had two further detailed discussions with him. After consulting Adrian Fortescue, who was to be my Chef de Cabinet and whose experience of Community matters extended right back to the time we first joined the Community – he had been a member of Christopher Soames' *Cabinet* – and whose knowledge, experience and diplomatic skill was to prove invaluable and Paolo Cecchini, who was to be a source of great support to me once we embarked on the structuring of what became the Internal Market Programme, I put it to Jacques Delors that if we were to make a success of this it was essential that we had a properly structured programme covering all the vital elements of the Internal Market. It was no good proceeding as previous Commissions had done, by simply picking out what were thought to be "priorities" or subjects which had happened to catch the eye of a particular Member State. It had to be the lot – a complete programme – where there was a clearly expressed intention to achieve the goal of creating a Europe which, in the words of the earliest of the Directives, operated as a single integrated market without frontiers or barriers in just the same way as the domestic market of an individual Member State. If this was to be achieved, I said, I needed control of all the major elements which went into the "Completion of the Internal Market". Not just the Internal Market portfolio as traditionally understood – which constituted the most important part of DG (Directorate General) III – but also the financial institutions and company taxation – the major part of DGXV – the Customs Union, which at that time was free standing, and indirect taxation, at that time the remaining part of DGXV. (The Customs Union and indirect taxation were subsequently merged to form a new DG, namely DGXXI.) It was, I said, impossible for me, if I was to complete the job properly and quickly, to be put in the position of having to argue with other Commissioners and their officials. I would produce the programme: I would consult in such detail as I thought necessary: I would present the programme to the Commission: they could then accept it, modify it or reject it. But I was not prepared to get bogged down in a bureaucratic mess: I was, I said, not simply or primarily a politician: I had run a major British company and I had run it successfully: this was that sort of job and that was the way I wanted to run it.

At this stage Jacques Delors noted what I had said but did not comment in any detail. He seemed much more interested in probing my thoughts than revealing his own. It was a reasonable enough attitude as he had 12 (as it then was) other Commissioners to see and he did not want to appear committed to any particular solution. But at our next meeting in Brussels he astounded me by offering me not just what I had asked for, but much more. In addition to everything else, he wanted me to take virtually the whole of DGIII, that is industry as well as the Internal Market. Hitherto "industry", which included coal and steel, an immense task in itself, as well as the whole range of other industries, had been a subject on its own and had been the "core" of another Commissioner's portfolio. What lay behind the offer was a judgement on his part that the Commission would progressively be less and less concerned with the "traditional" industries and that in future the "Industry" Commissioner should concentrate on the future, on research and development, the new technologies and the new industries.

I had not the slightest intention of being lumbered with coal and steel and to have taken what I had been offered would have presented an impossible workload. But I was conscious of the fact that hard bargaining might lie ahead before portfolios had been settled with all the Commissioners and that it would be extremely valuable to have something that I could concede with good grace in order to reach agreement. So I accepted. When I returned to London I was pressed very strongly by my own Department and by the Department of Industry to hold on to coal and steel. I made no reply for fear that anything I said might find its way back to Brussels and that the ploy I had in mind would be defeated.

But having, very quickly, reached agreement with Jacques Delors on my portfolio we then turned to the question of my approach to the subject. I said I wanted to follow the British precedent and at the earliest moment publish a "White Paper" setting out our programme in detail. To a Frenchman the term, and indeed the concept of a White Paper was novel: it was translated into "*Libre Blanc*" and then retranslated back into English as "White Book" and in Continental Europe it is still commonly referred to as the "White Book". (Interestingly, the term

"White Paper" has now passed into European terminology: thus the document on "Growth, Competitiveness and Unemployment" recently produced by the Commission in response to a request by the Heads of Government at the Edinburgh Summit is described as a "White Paper".) The White Paper should set out the philosophy or principles to be followed and the programme in detail. This must be a complete programme and it should be set in a time frame, every single proposal having its own time schedule and a completion time set for the whole project. In short, I proposed planning and executing the programme in precisely the same way as I had done in the past with an industrial project. We agreed that the target date should be "1992". My own rationale for this date was perfectly clear and I explained it to the Commission right at the very outset. The Treaty of Rome itself provided that the Customs Union which was the cornerstone of the common market, itself the foundation of the Community, should be completed over three periods of four years each, namely 12 years in all. "Four years" was the lifetime of a Commission and as each "Commission" has its own identity and commonly a different President and different membership, it provided a convenient measuring rod. The Customs Union was completed in 10½ years, well ahead of time. I argued that what our forebears could do nearly 30 years ago we should today be able to do at least as well and hopefully better. On this basis we should take two Commissions or eight years. Counting from January 1985 when we would take up office, this would take us to 31 December 1992. And that, I argued, should be our date. The line of reasoning I have set out above has now become the accepted explanation for the date chosen. Jacques Delors himself had also arrived at the "1992" date but by a different route and with a different definition as to what "1992" really meant. In the early days of the Commission I was involved in a dispute with Jacques Delors' *Cabinet* over precisely this point. His *Cabinet* was drafting documents on the basis of 1 January 1992. I said it meant and must mean 31 December 1992. In the end I won the argument. But from time to time the position is now confused by people with no knowledge of the background re-interpreting 1992 to mean 1993. I have always stongly opposed this, not simply because it is wrong, but because any reference to "1993" is an open invitation to footdraggers to re-interpret "1993" to mean 31 December 1993. In the end the matter was put beyond all doubt by the very specific wording of the Single European Act which referred to the programme being completed "progressively over a period expiring on 31 December 1992".

There will always be argument over who "invented" 1992. Interestingly, Jacques Delors himself posed this question in the article he contributed to the July 1990 issue of the *Kangaroo News* (the newspaper of the Kangaroo Group of the European Parliament founded by Boz Ferranti); but while he posed the question he did not answer it. I suspect that the truth of the matter is that all sorts of people had proposed all sorts of dates – just as their definition of what needed to be done equally varied. Thus Wisse Dekker, the President of Phillips, had been a tireless campaigner for 1990 – a date I felt was unrealistic.

My own view is that the final choice of "1992" emerged as I have indicated in the conversations I had with Jacques Delors in the autumn of 1984. What I can say with complete confidence is that by the time the Commission met formally in January 1985, "1992" was firmly on the agenda although it was not until my dispute with Jacques Delors *Cabinet* had been resolved in my favour that it was accepted that "1992" meant 31 December 1992. This then appeared specifically and, publicly for the first time, in Jacques Delors' speech to the European Parliament on 15 March 1985.

But while I had now reached very clear agreement with Jacques Delors himself we still had to face the hurdle of the first full – but legally "informal" – meeting of the new Commission. This took place on 7 December 1984 in the monastery of Royaumont used by the French Government as a venue for important meetings and situated just outside Paris.

Royaumont was to set the pattern for many subsequent "weekends of reflection" which Jacques Delors was to hold during his Presidency of the Commission. However attractive the venue, the weather was appalling and it was in this damp and soggy atmosphere that what was to prove one of the most historic of all the Commissions which had held office since the foundation of the Community met for the first time. Some of us had already met: but for others it was our first meeting. Jacques Delors had done his preparatory work with skill and thoroughness and initially the allocation of portfolios was agreed virtually without discussion. There was trouble to come: but for the moment he concentrated on discussing how he intended running the Commission. This was before the accession of Spain and Portugal and there were then 14 Commissioners including Jacques Delors himself: of these, three were hung over from the previous Commission, the other 11, including myself, were "new boys". In discussion, or argument, Jacques Delors therefore had very much his own way.

It was only as the day wore on that Karl-Heinz Narjes – or possibly more accurately his Chef de Cabinet, Heinrich von Moltke, for whom I subsequently developed the highest regard and indeed friendship – realised that his portfolio as "Industry Commissioner" was very different from what he had anticipated. It would of course have been better had the traditional title been dropped in favour of a more accurate description, but Jacques Delors no doubt felt that that would have provoked conflict. Karl-Heinz Narjes tried repeatedly to have the dividing line between his responsibilities and mine redefined in a way which would have left him in effective control of iron and steel and the whole of the traditional industries in addition to Research, Science and Technology which was the kernel of the portfolio Jacques Delors had already agreed with him. Finally at 2.30 a.m. in the morning I agreed to surrender iron and steel. Jacques Delors was greatly relieved at what he felt was flexibility and a *communautaire* spirit on my part. He declared the matter settled and the Minutes were written accordingly. A long rearguard action was fought by Karl-Heinz Narjes. He refused to agree the Minutes. I simply took the view that the decision had been taken and decisions cannot be altered by trying to rewrite the Minutes. In the end a *modus vivendi* was reached under which we were asked to "co-operate" with one another which meant that I retained those industries in which I had a specific interest or which I thought were especially important from the Internal Market point of view: these included, for example, the food industry, chemicals and pharmaceuticals, wholesale and retail distribution, the textile industry and the construction industry. Karl-Heinz Narjes took the lead on automobiles, ship building and engineering, in addition of course to coal and steel which I had earlier conceded. None of this had any relevance to my responsibility for Internal Market aspects extending over the whole field including those industries which *de facto* were allocated to Karl-Heinz Narjes. Thus "standards" were my responsibility although most standards relate to engineering. Despite the theoretical imperfection of these arrangements I was more than happy with the situation as it relieved me of responsibility for many problems which had no relationship to the Internal Market and which would have taken time which could be much better spent getting on with the job of achieving the completion of the Internal Market.

In many respects my success in the portfolio negotiations marked the high watermark of my relations with the Prime Minister. I had secured everything that really mattered to the United Kingdom, particularly the financial institutions as well as the Internal Market and I had done this without the need for "political" intervention, that is the need for the Head of Government to intervene with the President of the Commission. The weekend before we went to Brussels formally to take up my new duties, my wife and I had lunch at Chequers with Mrs Thatcher and Denis; the other guest was Norman Tebbit who was then recovering from the appalling injuries he had received in the bombing of the Grand Hotel. We were meeting in the warm afterglow of the Fontainebleau Summit. It was this period I had in mind when I spoke in the House of Lords the day after Mrs Thatcher's downfall when I referred to: "the happier times of years gone by". That afternoon all was sweetness and light: the storm was yet to come.

## Chapter 4

# The Forging of the Internal Market Programme

## Writing the White Paper

I left the British Cabinet in September 1984 immediately my appointment to the Commission was announced. But I retained my rooms in the Cabinet Office and I had a period of four months which I could devote to studying the problems that "Completion of the Internal Market" would involve and how best these problems could be met. Much of what I decided is reflected in the account I have given above of my discussions with Jacques Delors. I was, frankly, horrified at the paucity of the briefing I had received from the Departments concerned. It was moreover excessively concerned with budgetary matters, expenditure on the Common Agricultural Policy, budget discipline, own resources and the British budget contribution and all this despite the fact that what were then thought to be satisfactory solutions to all those problems had been reached a few months earlier at Fontainbleau. The clearest possible indication of the fixation on these matters and the very lowly position held by the Internal Market in the pecking order of matters needed to be considered is devastatingly revealed by the fact that the main policy briefing produced for Jacques Delors' visit to London in October

1984 extended to nine pages: the section on the Internal
Market occupied seven lines. In another briefing document the following extraordinary statement about the Internal Market appeared:

> "The current Commission [*i.e.* the Thorn Commission then
> reaching the end of its term of office] has repeatedly called
> for progress over an unrealistically wide front. More focus is
> needed."

The trouble was precisely the opposite: namely that the
scope of the proposals was too narrow, not too wide: the
vision needed to be extended over the whole field, not
"focussed" or constricted to a limited number of issues.

I have re-read afresh what I was then given. My reaction
to it today is that it reflects so clearly what since has regret-
tably been my diagnosis of the attitude of politicians in
our own country to the Community: they recall little of its
history, know nothing of its philosophy; and even more
striking is the virtually complete absence of hard, factual
knowledge. Perhaps the most trenchant criticism of all is
that they were and remain unaware of these deficiencies.

I have already referred to the two major conclusions I
had reached and agreed with Jacques Delors: namely that
it should be a "complete" programme and that it should
be set in a time frame. But I now came to two further
conclusions. First, that it must be set in a philosophical
framework. It was only this which would give the programme real momentum, would capture people's imagination, would generate the enthusiasm which alone
would guarantee success. We not only needed to know
*what* to do: we must know *why* we were doing it. Secondly,
we must find a new approach which broke away from the
familiar litany of "goods, services, people and capital".
This was not simply a search for novelty. It was intended

also to demonstrate that while we might be looking at old problems, we were looking at them in a new way. That we offered the prospect of success, not a repeat of the failures of the past. And that above all we had a single, coherent vision of the kind of Europe we wanted to achieve.

The essence of this new approach quite simply was this. If you ask yourself the apparently naive question "Why is there not freedom of movement?", the apparently naive answer is "Because there are obstacles or barriers". If one then asks oneself "What are these barriers?" one finds in a remarkable number of cases that they are the same, whether one is looking at goods or services, people or capital. The obvious conclusion therefore was that one ought not to be looking at freedom of movement *as such* and certainly not at goods, services, people and capital *separately* but at the obstacles or barriers which prevented that freedom of movement, irrespective of whether they concerned goods, services, people or capital. In short, one cut right through from "cause" to what the logicians called the *causa causans.*

Let me illustrate this in two important respects. The free circulation, or free movement, of goods is obstructed as often as not by differences in standards which form the basis of technical regulations relating to health and safety and increasingly to the environment and consumer protection. If one looks at the barriers which affect the freedom of circulation of financial services they are as often as not differences in regulatory requirements, both prudential requirement and measures to protect the consumer. Essentially therefore the obstacles or barriers are the same, whether one is looking at goods or services. There was an enormous UK interest here because of our major stake in the service industries. Once one could demonstrate that there was no essential difference between goods and services one broke down the psychological barriers that had led to progress on "goods" and stagnation on "services". It opened up the way to applying the "New Approach to Standards" which we had begun to develop in the case of goods following the *Cassis de Dijon* judgment, to services. Briefly, one harmonised at Community level only the "essential requirements" and once this had been done there would be mutual recognition of national standards and a legal right of freedom of circulation. And on the argument I now put forward one could apply this to services as well as goods. This was one of the great breakthroughs in attitude and approach made in the White Paper and a development in which I have taken particular personal pride. The "New Approach to Standards" was set out in a Commission Communication dated 7 May 1985. It was in a sense a precursor of the White Paper on the Internal Market which was to come the following month.

In the first serious trial run of the "New Approach", namely in the field of pressure vessels – an odd choice unless one remembers that a pressure vessel designed to inadequate standards can explode and cause serious loss of life – we reduced the Community legislation required from an estimated 500 pages – ten Directives of 50 pages each – needed under the old system to five pages under the New Approach. So much for Brussels bureaucracy. It was a parallel but different approach from the much trumpeted "subsidiarity" under the Maastricht Treaty and likely ultimately to prove a more appropriate and more successful one.

My other illustration relates to frontiers and frontier controls. So very often – indeed one might say "invariably" – the freedom of movement of goods and persons, and to some extent capital, is obstructed by frontier controls. "Frontiers" are necessary as demarcation lines between the territory of one state and the territory of another. But increasingly and substantially they have attracted controls designed to enforce plant and veterinary health regulations, the conformity of goods to technical regulations relating to health and safety and other matters, immigration controls, measures against terrorists, drug traffickers and international criminals and perhaps most important of all they have become the point at which taxes are collected or refunded. The frontiers and the frontier controls have become the most blatant manifestation of a Europe which remains divided. If the Community was to become a United Europe, however one defines "United", the frontiers and the controls associated with them would have to go. It is useless simplifying the controls and leaving the frontiers in place. As long as the frontiers are there they will attract controls: each control will be the excuse for some other control. And we would soon find ourselves back in the same position as we were before the White Paper was launched.

It was for all of these reasons that when I came to write the White Paper, I decided that the approach must be one of cutting right through the undergrowth and looking directly at the barriers or obstacles. This is why the White Paper is structured in terms of "Physical Barriers", "Technical Barriers" and "Fiscal Barriers". It is also why the "frontiers" and the removal of the frontiers became such an important, if not the most important, part of the philosophy of "Completion of the Internal Market". And why when the Single European Act came to be drafted the "Completion of the Internal Market" was defined in terms of "an area without internal frontiers".

I am perhaps running a little ahead of my main story. During the early winter of 1984, before the new

Commission took up duty, I had discussions in Brussels with the key figures who were to form the team which would draw up the Programme for the Completion of the Internal Market and then to drive it through to success. Pre-eminent was Fernand Braun, the Luxembourger who was Director General of DGIII, the Directorate General which was to play the lead role. He was a man of immense experience and unrivalled knowledge of the way the Community and the Commission in particular operated. But of critical importance he was immensely influential in the Commission Services and perhaps one of the best known personalities in the Community. His Assistant Director General in DGIII was Paolo Cecchini who subsequently achieved fame as the author of the Cecchini Report which was to analyse in the most convincing way the benefits of the Internal Market Programme. He was a personal friend of Adrian Fortescue, my Chef de Cabinet, and he did more than anyone to prepare me for the forthcoming negotiations on the allocation of the Commission portfolios which I have already described in Chapter 3. I made contact also with Bus Henriksen, the Dane, who was Director General of DGXV which was responsible for the financial services, company law and taxation, and indirect taxes; and Friedrich Klein, the German Director General in charge of the Customs Union. So well before I took up my duties I had firmly established my lines of communication and ensured that I would have a team firmly committed to achieving our objective. It was only years afterwards that Fernand Braun said to me that I had given my Services a clear objective and unambiguous leadership and at long last and for the first time for many years, he said, they knew exactly what was expected of them.

One trivial event occurred which for me, at any rate, cast the clearest light on the problems I was to meet and did more than anything else to shape the way that ultimately I faced the problems which were to confront me. During one of my visits to the headquarters of the Commission, I was told that Gaston Thorn, the retiring President of the Commission, wanted to see me. He spent the whole of the time I was with him complaining bitterly that his period of office as President had been ruined by the dispute over the British budget contribution. "Of course", he said, "you were right. But it is no good being right if the other nine [as it then was] are against you". It was a tragic epitaph on a wasted four years. But to me it was also a warning for the future.

We took up duty as the new Commission on 6 January 1985. We met formally the following day which was a Monday: but the first full meeting of the Commission was on 9 January. I had already expressed some general views on how I proposed tackling the question of the Internal Market at the meeting in December at Royaumont. Delors had also paved the way by inducing the Heads of Government when they met in Dublin in December 1984 to ask

"the Council in its appropriate formations . . . [to] take steps to complete the Internal Market."

The part played by the European Council, that is the meetings of the Heads of Government, is of critical importance in establishing the broad policies the Community is to follow. But in fact the problem so often is that the "conclusions" of the Heads of Government are an endorsement of the policies the Commission, which legally enjoys the sole right of initiative, puts to them. The value of such an endorsement is obvious. Now, at two full meetings of the Commission, I fleshed out my ideas and my approach on the lines I have already described. But there was one further point I added. It was, I said, essential that we should base our individual proposals on what we thought was right: not what we thought the Member States would accept; whatever proposals the Commission put to the Council of Ministers were bound to be watered down; if we started with what we thought was acceptable, by the time the Council had done their worst we would be left with weak and ineffectual measures; far better to start with what was right even if it meant long and protracted battles with the Council: that way we would stand at least a chance of ending up with something that was effective if far from perfect. This approach was vehemently supported by Peter Sutherland, the Irish Commissioner in charge of competition, but otherwise there was little or no discussion and the point was accepted. The decision was entirely right and perhaps more than anything ensured that we would end up with an effective, working Single Market and be spared the disappointments and ineffectiveness of much of what had happened in the previous 30 years. But it was also to be the source of long and hard fought battles and much deliberate misrepresentation by governments and special interest lobbies determined to maintain the status quo.

There was another issue which first peered above the parapet at this stage but was to cause trouble and difficulty throughout the lifetime of the Commission and has still not disappeared. That is the question of "linkage". The poorer Member States, that is mainly those in the South but including Ireland which I always regarded as an honorary Mediterranean country, argued tenaciously that the Completion of the Internal Market would be primarily for the benefit of the advanced industrial Member States of the North and that the poorer Member States in the South should be compensated to ensure greater "economic convergence" – one of the accepted policies of the

Community. The ranks of the Southern Member States were greatly strengthened when, the following year, they were joined by Spain and Portugal. The compensation claimed ultimately took the form of a massive increase in the various "Structural Funds", primarily the regional fund and the social fund, or through special programmes such as those ultimately negotiated for Greece (IMPS) or Portugal (PEDIP).

I regarded the argument in the way that it was put as nonsense on the ground that the increase in prosperity that the Internal Market Programme would produce would benefit the South just as much as the North through an increase in demand for their products: and that if one looked at industry in particular the effect would be for industry to migrate from the North with its high costs to the South with its much lower level of costs. Experience was to prove that this analysis was correct. Nevertheless I accepted that if the less developed countries of the South were to be able to take full advantage of the new opportunities opened up it was essential that both the human and the physical infrastructure of those regions should be greatly strengthened. The agreement I made with my colleagues from the South was that in return for their support for my Internal Market Programme, I would support them in their demands that the Structural Funds should be doubled. But "linkage" I would not accept at any price. (I illustrated my argument by reference to the old Music Hall turn "After you Cecil: after you Claude". Because they could not agree whether Cecil or Claude should go first, neither in fact moved.) I argued that if we tried to make progress on the Internal Market dependent on progress in the regions, neither would make progress. But if we allowed the Internal Market Programme to go ahead unhindered, it would provide the increased prosperity to pay for increases in the Structural Funds. Success in one area was the best guarantee for success elsewhere. While this agreement held firm in the Commission, repeated efforts were made both in the Council of Ministers and to some extent in the European Council to establish linkage. But I succeeded in fighting it off. Ultimately the success of the line I had taken was sealed by the fact that at the second Brussels Summit in February 1988 when the success of the Internal Market Programme was clear, the Heads of Government agreed to doubling the Structural Funds. It is worth recalling that once again this was bitterly opposed by the United Kingdom. They wanted the Single Market but they were not prepared to pay for it. But once again they were faced down by the other 11 Member States.

There is one further aspect of this matter which is worth mentioning. In the end I produced my programme and it was endorsed by the Heads of Government in less than six months. It was more than three years before agreement was reached on the Structural Funds. And on social policy, the other main area in which demands for "linkage" were put forward, it took more than four years before the Social Charter saw the light of day. Had "linkage" been accepted it would have resulted in intolerable delay being imposed on the Internal Market Programme and in the light of subsequent changes in the economic and political climate this delay could well have frustrated the programme altogether.

The Commission is a collegiate body. Although Commissioners each have their own portfolio, the whole Commission has to agree with all action which is taken in the name and under the authority of the Commission. The secret of success, to have one's proposals accepted by the Commission without undue argument, lies in securing the prior agreement of the Chefs de Cabinet. The "*Cabinet*" system which is unknown in this country is part of the accepted political structure on the Continent. A *Cabinet* is usually at a higher level and is much more influential than a Minister's Private Office is in this country. Not uncommonly members of a *Cabinet*, and particularly the Chef de Cabinet, will stay with an individual whether he is in Office or in Opposition. There tends therefore to be a degree of closeness between a Minister or Commissioner and his Chef de Cabinet unlike anything one finds in this country and a good Chef will "know" his Minister's or Commissioner's mind and will accept a great deal of responsibility on his behalf. The Commission works very much in this way and the part played by the Chefs de Cabinet is critical to the smooth and effective working of the Commission. Normally they "prepare" meetings of the Commission in advance. That is, they go through the agenda and see to what extent prior agreement can be reached and, if not, to identify the points of disagreement. Where prior agreement among the Chefs is reached, the item still appears on the Commission's agenda but it is described as an "A" point and it is formally agreed without further discussion. If an item is not so designated it is discussed but discussion is limited – or ought to be limited – to the points identified by the Chefs. If agreement can be reached that is the end of the matter: if not, the item will be referred back and will return to the Commission at a later date. Ultimately in the absence of agreement a vote is taken. The vote is by simple majority but it must be a majority of the whole Commission, not simply of those present. This meant that with 17 Commissioners it was necessary to secure nine positive votes if an item was disputed.

It was a remarkable achievement on the part of Adrian Fortescue, my Chef de Cabinet, who had a long experience in these matters, that following the preliminary and very general discussions which had taken place in January to which I have already referred, he was able to secure virtually total agreement among the Chefs de Cabinet both to the White Paper and to the 300 proposals it contained before the matter was referred to the Commission again. A programme which could easily have taken very many months, if not years, to secure agreement within the Commission was accepted after only two further discussions and even those discussions were confined to two important issues. The first concerned attempts by other Commissioners to "hitch a ride" on the Internal Market Programme: the second to further attempts to create linkage between the Internal Market Programme and additional assistance for the poorer Member States. The first point related primarily to competition policy and to transport. There is of course a valid argument that progress in both these areas was essential if the full benefits of an integrated market were to be achieved. But at the same time this could be said of an enormous range of other policies and if all these arguments were to be accepted, the programme would become so overloaded that its chances of success would be prejudiced. But some concession had to be made and to include some reference in the White Paper both to competition policy and to transport policy and this was necessary to avoid the risk of a delay which could have put back the whole programme. On "linkage" the only change made was to spell out the need to take action in the regional and social field in parallel with progress on the Internal Market.

My aim throughout had been to put the White Paper to the Heads of Government in time for their endorsement when they met at Milan on the 28 and 29 of June that year (1985). The drafting of the White Paper was completed by

the beginning of June and Commission endorsement secured but it was not sent to the Heads of Government
until 14 June and they probably did not receive it until a
few days later. This timing was not without deliberate intent. It gave the Heads of Government sufficient time to
read the document and appreciate the immense importance of the opportunity being opened up. But it did not
give their officials time to pick it to pieces. In the hope of
making certainty more certain, I prefaced the White Paper by a series of quotations from the Conclusions of previous Summits to fix in the minds of the Heads of
Government that it was just what they had been asking for.
I had hoped to go further and include photographs of the
individual Heads of Government with a quotation from
each. But the constraint of time frustrated this.

I realised too that favourable press coverage was essential to success. We decided therefore that a major press
conference must be held. Jacques Delors insisted I should
take it. It was an act of generosity as he could so easily, as
President of the Commission, have tried to take the credit
himself. I decided to prepare the ground. Jacques Delors
had always been upset by the amount of leaking to the
press which was occurring from the Commission, the
source of which was suspected but could never be
positively identified. But I decided I would take the risk
and do what others were doing. This was the time when
the British Government was beginning to develop leaking
into an art form as an arm of government policy. I decided
therefore to send the *Financial Times* advance copies of the
White Paper and invite them into my office for a detailed
briefing not just of the proposals but of the philosophy
underlying them. The *Financial Times* maintained total se-
crecy. There was no leak but we got very full and well
informed coverage. The press conference when it was

held on Saturday, 15 June 1985 was equally a complete success.

There was extensive and extremely favourable coverage in the press throughout the whole of Europe. The British press was almost unanimous in its support. The *Financial Times* commented:

> "The White Paper invites the forthcoming Milan Summit to define the goal as nothing less than the removal of all intra-European frontier formalities by 1992. Then with remorseless logic it spells out the consequences. 'They asked for it. They've got it' says the zealous new internal market commissioner Lord Cockfield."

In the leader, the *Financial Times* says:

> "Lord Cockfield's White Paper underlines the political incentive. There is no area in which progress where it can be made would be more visible a move directly relevant to the aims, ambitions and visions of the Community."

And it concluded:

> "There are two compelling reasons why the White Paper deserves support. The first is that the European economy needs shock therapy if it is to hold its own [in the world]. . . . The second is that the Commission has rightly exploded the fallacy that Europe can somehow enjoy the benefits of a market of 320m people without substantial concessions of national sovereignty . . . the European Community needs a clear and pragmatic goal and the Commission has provided a worthy one."

*The Times* described the White Paper as:

> "a prodigious work programme."

*The Guardian* commented:

> "the Cockfield document presents the summit with the chance of fundamental progress."

*The Daily Telegraph* wrote:

> "Announcing the White Paper on Saturday Lord Cockfield, former Trade Secretary now EEC Commissioner for Internal Trade said it would 'fundamentally alter the face of Europe for the rest of our lifetime' ",

and it went on to say:

> "The free trade aspects of the proposals will be welcomed by the Government."

*Les Echos* in Paris described it as:

> "A programme for a Utopia."

*The Scotsman* referred to:

> "the formidable White Paper produced by Lord Cockfield",

and went on to say:

> "Lord Cockfield's proposals have laid down a challenge to Europe and its leaders."

It commented:

> "The proposals are so far reaching that French journalists accredited to the EEC who have grown accustomed to lukewarm British commitment to Europe were left bemused at the scope and detail of the Cockfield plan."

And a few months later *The Guardian* was to say:

> "Lord Cockfield, Britain's most popular export to Europe for years."

I have quoted primarily from the British press but the comment throughout the Community was equally positive and massively supportive.

The launch of the White Paper established the Programme for the Completion of the Internal Market as a vital and imaginative giant step forward for the Community and I have no doubt that this contributed to the overwhelming endorsement the programme was to receive a few days afterwards from the Heads of Government when they met at Milan.

The Conclusions of the Summit read as follows:

> "The Council welcomed the White Paper on completing the internal market submitted . . . by the Commission" and "it instructed the Council [of Ministers] to initiate a precise programme of action based on the White Paper . . . with a view to achieving completely and effectively the conditions for a single market in the Community by 1992 at the latest in accordance with . . . a binding timetable."

Note in particular the phrases "achieving completely and effectively" and "by 1992 at the latest" and finally "a binding timetable".

These criteria, soon to be reflected in the terms of the Single European Act to which I will come in the next Chapter, were crucial to the success of the programme.

In this way the Internal Market Programme emerged as the "Flagship of the Enterprise", a position which was to be entrenched and indeed enhanced as time went on and other policies in which so much hope had been invested, fell by the wayside. It is interesting to trace the events which brought this position of preeminence about.

I have already made the point that the Internal Market occupied a very subordinate place in the Solemn Declaration signed at Stuttgart in June 1983 and that it had disappeared altogether from the conclusions of the Fontainebleau Summit in June of the following year. It remained of course an important item on the agenda but, while as far as I was concerned it occupied centre stage and was the sole reason for my going to Brussels, even in

Jacques Delors' order of priorities it ranked well behind his plans for Economic and Monetary Union and strengthening the roles and powers of the European Parliament. Interestingly, in his first speech as President to the Parliament on 14 January 1985 in setting out the main lines of policy to be followed by the new Commission of which he was President ("The Thrust of Commission Policy") the greater part of the speech is occupied by matters of broad political philosophy. It is not until about half way through the speech that he refers to the "decisive steps" the Commission proposed to take "in these directives". These comprise: "a large market and industrial co-operation", the "strengthening of the European Monetary System" and the "convergence of economies". On the basis we had agreed in the discussions that took place in the previous autumn, he then went on to say "A programme, a timetable and a method will be proposed to Council and Parliament". But he gave no details: there was at that stage no reference to "1992" despite the fact that it had featured so prominently in our own discussions.

His "inaugural speech" as it would now be called, was followed up by a further speech to the Parliament on 12 March 1985 introducing the Commission's Work Programme for 1985. In this speech Jacques Delors said: "I propose to concentrate on four issues . . .".

The first issue was "*enlargement*". The second was the promotion of a "*strong and active Europe*" and under this heading Jacques Delors discussed *inter alia* monetary problems and the "*promotion . . . [of] the ECU as as international reserve asset*". The Internal Market does not appear until the "*third issue*" and even then it is only one item in a list of measures – "*The third issue I would like to discuss is the importance of Europe regaining its econ-*

*omic vigour . . .*''. A Community-wide market was included under this heading together with: ''*High technology as an element in Europe's competitiveness*'' and ''*Revival of the social dialogue*''.

I have gone into this detail simply to make the point that ''Completion of the Internal Market'' was at the outset no more than one of a large number of measures designed to breathe new life into what had become a moribund Community – important but ranking well behind grand projects such as Economic and Monetary Union. What therefore explains why it soon became what I have described as ''the Flagship of the Enterprise''? Promoted in the Single Act from the humble position it occupied in the Solemn Declaration to pole position in the Single European Act? And now widely regarded as the main achievement of the decade in which Jacques Delors was President of the Commission?

The answer was furnished, long before the event and in a different context by Shakespeare:

> ''There is a tide in the affairs of men, which taken at the flood leads to success.''

There was indeed a tide which had begun to flow in 1983 when the Solemn Declaration was signed: and it was the sheer speed with which I produced the White Paper setting out the Single Market Programme which enabled ''the tide'' to be ''taken at the flood''. The new Commission took up duty on 6 January 1985: the White Paper with details of its 300 proposals was sent to the Heads of Government on 14 June of the same year – five months, one week and one day. While possibly not the first time in recorded history that so massive, so important, so detailed a policy could have been produced in so short a time, it could have had few equals and certainly none in the lifetime of the European Community. If one looks at the other major policies to which the Community and the Commission had turned its hand, Economic and Monetary Union was not fleshed out until the Treaty of Maastricht was signed six years later; the programme on the Structural Funds was only agreed in February 1988, three years after the Commission had taken office; and the Social Charter did not see the light of day until May 1989 when a new Commission had taken office and still occupies an uncomfortable place in or only appended to the Maastricht Treaty. In short, when the White Paper setting out the Programme for the Completion of the Internal Market appeared, there were no rivals to attract attention, the White Paper took centre stage; indeed it was the only player on the stage. It was of course a programme of immense scope and imagination. We succeeded in selling it well. The fact that the seed fell on fertile soil cannot in any way distract from the magnificent efforts and the great achievement of all those who contributed to the programme and were to work valiantly together to drive it through to ultimate and complete success.

On a less happy note, the publication of the White Paper marked the first days in the deterioration of my relations with the Prime Minister (Mrs Thatcher). I had seen her when the White Paper was still in draft to let her know the lines on which I was thinking and what progress was being made. In particular I explained why I was departing from the traditional approach of "goods, services, persons and capital" and structuring the White Paper in terms of "barriers" to the freedom of movement, namely the physical barriers, the technical barriers and the fiscal barriers. I sensed that the reference to "fiscal barriers" was ill-received. I saw the Prime Minister again immediately after the publication of the White Paper. I told her that I appreciated the political sensitivity of tax harmonization particularly in relation to the VAT zero rates. I explained to her that I had taken every possible step to cushion the position for the United Kingdom. I had departed from the traditional approach of "harmonization" and had proposed only "approximation" within broad bands: it would not be until 1992 that approximation would need to be completed: and finally in relation to zero rates I had said not once, not twice, but three times in the White Paper that there would be particular difficulties in this field and derogations might be needed. Sensing that all was not well I said that I had not invented harmonization of indirect taxation, it was accepted Community policy long before we joined the Community and indeed was specifically provided for in the Treaty of Rome. The following conversation then took place.

Myself:  It was in the Treaty of Rome.
The PM: It was not.
Myself:  It was.
The PM: It was not.
Myself:  It was.

This unproductive conversation was brought to an end by the Private Secretary being sent to find a copy of the Treaty of Rome. I asked him to read out Article 99, which reads as follows:

"The Commission shall present proposals for the harmonization of indirect taxes . . .".

This was greeted in complete silence. I was to learn over the years that silence was always the Prime Minister's response when in difficulties. But thinking as I then did that it was possible to penetrate this iron defence I said:

Myself:  You ought to have read it before you signed it.

The PM: I didn't sign it.

Myself:   I know you didn't. But you were a member of the Cabinet which did sign it.

Silence.


So that was the note on which we parted. I was to learn over the years that the Prime Minister's hard knowledge of European matters was somewhat lacking. And that when at a loss, in Burke's words she "depended on her imagination for her facts".

The UK's position on indirect taxation was indeed a great deal weaker than I had indicated even in my discussions with the Prime Minister. The VAT, for example, was established as the Community's sole turnover tax by two Directives adopted as long ago as 11 April 1967 and it was required to be levied on a common basis. We were bound under the Treaty of Accession to accept this. The zero rates at the time we introduced them were almost certainly illegal and they were only legitimised *post facto*, and legally on a temporary basis, as part of the bargaining which led up to the adoption of the Sixth VAT Directive in 1977: and more recently the Court of Justice has struck down some of the zero rates as going beyond even the latitude given by the Sixth VAT Directive. The furore created when Mr Norman Lamont, who had by then become Chancellor of the Exchequer, agreed in June 1991 on a binding minimum rate of VAT illustrates how little people have learned in the 20 years since we signed the Treaty of Accession and joined the Community.

My troubles over indirect taxation were greatly exacerbated by press reports, no doubt inspired, which gave a most distorted view of my proposals. The zero rates, however essential they might be considered on "political" grounds, deprived the Treasury of huge amounts of revenue which could have been used to pursue other objectives and indeed a succession of Chancellors of the Exchequer had restricted the operation of the zero rates on revenue grounds and Nigel Lawson, who was Chancellor of the Exchequer at the time the Commission's proposals were published, was no exception. A vigorous press campaign was mounted denouncing the Commission for wanting to abolish the zero rates. This in fact was completely untrue. I had taken the precaution in paragraph 14 of the White Paper to say:

> "Approximation of indirect taxation will cause severe problems for some Member States. It may, therefore, be necessary to provide for derogations."

The point was driven home in paragraph 218 in which I said:

> ". . . the Commission recognises that the approximation of indirect taxation will give rise to considerable problems for some Member States; and that as a consequence it may be necessary to provide for derogations. There are areas of considerable political sensitivity which have to be accommodated in this way."

The point was repeated *ad nauseam* when the detailed proposals were published in August 1987.

In response to the press attention Nigel Lawson gave a categorical assurance to maintain the zero rate on *food.* The Prime Minister, however, went further and gave an unequivocal pledge to maintain *all* zero rates. She seemed to be unaware of the fact that successive Chancellors of the Exchequer had nibbled away at the zero rates and indeed were to continue to do so. But the effect of her intervention was to lock the United Kingdom once again into a situation which was bound to distance it from the other members of the Community. So far as I was concerned, it no doubt damaged my position in the United Kingdom but it greatly enhanced my standing in the Community as it established me as someone prepared to honour the obligations set out in the Treaty requiring Commissioners not to accept dictation by national governments and to do so irrespective of the pressures put upon them. Much as I regret having to say so, what emerged over the years was that the most powerful support I enjoyed in the Community was the Prime Minister's hostility.

# Chapter 5
# The Single European Act

French is the working language of the European Community. Its legal documents are always written in French in the first instance: they are then translated into the nine Community languages – there are only nine because the Belgians speak French and Dutch, the Luxembourgers use French or German and the Irish speak English. While all the texts have equal legal validity it is often valuable to go back to the French original. In the original text the document is called the *"Acte Unique"*. "Single Act" is an entirely correct translation but to an Englishman at any rate it sacrifices the glamour a phonetic translation – 'The Unique Act" – would convey.

It is called the *"Acte Unique"* or "Single Act" because in the early stages the possibility of a series of Acts, each covering one or more of the subjects under consideration, seemed the likely outcome. And particularly one Act covering matters of Community competence and a separate Act covering political co-operation in foreign affairs, which is not within the Community "competence" but takes the form of "co-operation" between the Member States *qua* Member States and not as members of the Community although in practice it is serviced by the Community institutions and is dealt with in the Foreign Affairs Council. Jacques Delors was adamant that there should be a "Single Act" and in the end he got his way. There are of course *three*, not one, European Communities – the original Coal and Steel Community, the Economic Community and the Atomic Energy Community. The institutions were merged, finally in 1967, but each legally has its own separate existence and its own Treaty. But since 1967 all three have operated as a single "European Community" – which the Maastricht Treaty has finally legitimised. So far as the "Community" as such is concerned, the Maastricht Treaty has taken a step backwards in adopting a "three pillars" approach. But in 1985 when the Single Act was under negotiation Jacques Delors was determined to ensure that the process of consolidation into a single Community should not be reversed by the new developments now contemplated and a series of new and separate Communities created leading not to "European Union" but to European *dis*union.

The Single Act had a double provenance. If the Internal Market Programme was to succeed it would be essential to move away from unanimity, the source of much of the paralysis in the Community, to majority voting. The tragedy of the past, the primary reason for the stagnation of the Community, lay in the fact that while the Treaties envisaged that after the "transitional period" which ended in 1967, or at the latest in 1973, the general rule should be majority voting, nevertheless the Council of Ministers virtually insisted on unanimity. This stemmed from the so-called "Luxembourg Compromise" to which I have already referred and which was adopted in 1966 after the clash with General de Gaulle.

The exact meaning and scope of the Luxembourg Compromise is much disputed but in effect it enabled a single Member State to "veto" a proposal if what it regarded as its "very important interests" were at stake. Had the "veto" been restricted to what truly were "very important interests", the harm it would have done would have been limited. Unfortunately the policy which developed on the back of the Luxembourg Compromise was to insist on unanimity virtually everywhere and for the Council of Ministers to continue their discussions in the vain hope that unanimity would emerge although the sanction to encourage or enforce unanimity, namely the threat of majority voting, had been removed. The basic problem of course it that a Minister who loses out in an argument has to justify his position to critics in his national Parliament and it is so much easier to come home reporting "triumph" in the sense of preserving the "national interest" by blocking a proposal however valuable the measure might have been in Community terms, than to have to face the criticism of having "sacrificed" "national interests" however transient or trivial those national interests were. It is a sad fact that the further you go down the Ministerial ladder, the more attenuated courage becomes and nowhere was this more obvious than in the Council of Ministers. This comes out so very clearly if one looks at the decisions – often bold and far-sighted – taken by the Heads of Government at the Summit (the European Council) compared with all too often the indifference, if not hostility, shown by Ministers when the same proposals reached the Council of Ministers.

Against this background, majority voting on Internal Market proposals was an absolute necessity if the programme was to be completed and completed on time as the Heads of Government at Milan were to demand. "Majority voting" required a Treaty amendment: the Treaty of Amendment required an Intergovernmental Conference. The Italian Government, which in June 1985 when the White Paper was presented and approved held the Presidency, proposed that this should be held in Luxembourg in December of the same year. Predictably, Mrs Thatcher tried to veto it. But she was supported only by Denmark and Greece. So the Intergovernmental Conference went ahead and reluctantly and grudgingly Mrs Thatcher decided to join in.

There is an interesting postscript to this story. In later years Mrs Thatcher was to claim that Britain had launched the Internal Market Programme. My only reaction was to say that so far as she was concerned her contribution consisted of trying to knock a hole in the bottom of the boat. The argument which had been advanced by the British Government was that if Member States would only act reasonably and restrict the use of the Luxembourg veto to genuine cases of vital national interest there was no need to amend the rules. But after the decision was taken and majority voting introduced on Internal Market matters, the British Government tried valiantly to frustrate its use not least by attempting to add Article 235, which requires unanimity, to the legal base of any proposal to which it objected. But the Court of Justice, in the *Hormones* case, would have none of it. So despite Mrs Thatcher's efforts, we did get majority voting and as a result we have now seen the successful completion of the Internal Market Programme.

The second limb of the provenance of the Single Act lay in the determination of Jacques Delors, with the vigorous support of Lorenzo Natali, the Italian Vice President, to seize the opportunity to incorporate in an amending Treaty the objectives of the Solemn Declaration on European Union signed in Stuttgart in June 1983. Lorenzo Natali had served in the previous Commission, and indeed in the one before that. He was a man of immense experience, of considerable influence in his own Member State and a committed supporter of "European Union" and particularly of the European Parliament of which he had been a member.

The "Solemn Declaration" was, at the end of the day, only a piece of paper: but the Single Act would be a Treaty amendment and it would have the force of law. I believe that so far as both Jacques Delors and Lorenzo Natali were concerned, "European Union" was the dominant issue. Nevertheless, in the end the Single Act put the Internal Market in pole position: and it was followed by the other policies agreed at Stuttgart, namely Economic and Monetary Union, Social Policy, Economic and Social Cohesion, Science and Technology, the Environment and finally Political Co-operation in the field of foreign policy. The Single Act also extended the powers of the European Parliament, most notably in the introduction of the "co-operation procedure" for Internal Market matters.

There has been some controversy on whether it was the Internal Market or European Union which was the driving force of the Single European Act. The answer lies very much in who you are and where you stand. For my part I try and avoid the question by saying as I have done earlier in this chapter that the Single Act had a dual provenance.

The Single European Act is immensely important both in constitutional and in legal terms. It clearly defined and gave legal backing to the policies which were to form the future development of the Community. There could be argument over detailed content but no longer could anyone legitimately argue that Economic and Monetary Union and Social Policy, for example, were not agreed and accepted Community policies to which effect must be given. To a considerable degree this has still not been taken on board by the British political establishment, still less by the media, as the arguments over the Maastricht Treaty vividly illustrate. I believe the underlying reason for this failure to understand the position lies in the fact that in the United Kingdom we do not have a written constitution and many of these matters appear strange if not incomprehensible to us. But to Continental countries which do have written constitutions, the procedures represented by the Treaties, and now the Single Act, were familiar territory. The difference comes out most starkly if one takes a specific instance such as Monetary Union: to the Continental countries the Single European Act concludes the matter: the procedures laid down, for example the use of Article 236, are there to give effect to it. To the British Government in the Thatcher era the Single Act was little more than a vague expression of intent and the procedures were the mechanism provided to frustrate that intention.

Specifically on the Internal Market, the Single Act not only gave the programme the backing of law but it contained two crucially important provisions in Article 8A.

First, it defined the Internal Market as:

"an area without internal frontiers in which the free movement of goods, persons, services and capital is ensured . . .".

Secondly, it says that this is to be achieved:

"progressively . . . over a period expiring on 31 December 1992 . . .".

Note how specific both these provisions are.

So far as the *definition* is concerned, note that it says "without internal frontiers": *not* simply with some controls abolished and/or simplified frontier procedures. The Act requires the total abolition of internal frontiers and by necessary implication the abolition of the frontier controls that go with internal frontiers.

So far as the *date* is concerned, the Act requires the programme to be completed by 31 December 1992. Not by some later date or by some unspecified date. The "progressively" of course means that measures do not necessarily all have to come into effect on 31 December 1992: some can come into force earlier and indeed the intention was that change should be a progressive operation spread over time to give Member States the opportunity to implement and digest the changes provided they all took effect by 31 December 1992 at the latest. Indeed some very important changes did indeed take effect well before 1992 – for example the liberalization of capital movements, the mutual recognition of professional qualifications and many of the Directives liberalising public procurement: but there are many other examples.

Perhaps I should deal with the numerous Declarations appended to the Single Act. There are two I would particularly pick out. The first of these refers to Article 8A and relates to the date of 31 December 1992 for the completion of the Internal Market Programme. The Declaration says that the article expresses the "firm political will" of the Member States "to complete the internal market" by that date and "more particularly [to take] the decisions necessary to implement the Commission's programme described in the White Paper on the Internal Market".

So far so good. The Heads of Government are saying these are no empty words: there is a firm and clear determination to achieve the programme.

But there is then a qualification. This is in the following form:

"Setting the date of 31 December 1992 does not create an automatic legal effect."

It is the precise meaning of this qualification and its legal effect I will discuss in a moment.

The second of the Declarations which I have singled out – and which might be referred to as the "Thatcher Declaration" because that is its source – reads:

"Nothing in these provisions [relating to the abolition of internal frontiers] shall affect the right of Member States to take such measures as they consider necessary for the purpose of controlling immigration from third countries, and to combat terrorism, crime, the traffic in drugs and illicit trading in works of art and antiques."

In English law declarations of this sort would have no effect. They would be regarded as no more than expressions of opinion which could not alter the plain words of the Statute. Continental law however is rather more flexible in its outlook and the probability is that the Court of Justice will tend to follow the European line.

Declarations of this kind are commonly inserted by Member States when legislation is agreed to provide a defence for Ministers in their home state when they have been outvoted; or to put down a marker for the future: or sometimes as a cloak to hide the Member State's intention to give its own and dubious interpretation to the legislative provisions. So far as the "Thatcher Declaration" is concerned there could be an element of all three. But what matters is not so much what was in the secret recesses of the promoter's mind but what the Court of Justice will make of it and there is now every indication that the matter will come to the Court. The European Parliament has already commenced proceedings against the Commission for its alleged failure to ensure the implementation of Article 8A and the United Kingdom may well intervene in these proceedings.

It is always a high risk to attempt to forecast what decision any court will make. Subject to this caveat, I suspect that so far as the first of the Declarations, that relating to the date of 31 December 1992 is concerned, the Court would tend to read this in conjunction with Article 100B. That article provides that where national provisions affecting the Internal Market have not been harmonised as Article 100A provides, the Commission shall in the course of 1992 draw up an inventory of such provisions, the Council should decide which can be dealt with under the "mutual recognition" principle and that for the rest the Commission should submit "appropriate proposals in good time to allow the Council to act before the end of 1992". The Declaration expresses a clear political determination to complete this process in good time and Article 100B provides the machinery to ensure that it is done. But it would perhaps be too much to expect the last "t" to be crossed and the last "i" to be dotted by midnight on 31 December 1992. The Declaration therefore is saying that the axe should not fall "automatically" on that date. A reasonable amount of elbow room should be given and if it was clear that both Commission and Council really were honestly and genuinely getting on with the job, they should be given a reasonable amount of latitude to comply. On this interpretation, the Declaration, even if it has any effect at all, does no more than provide reasonable flexibility if here and there some slippage does occur. The Commission themselves appear very much to have taken this line. But their patience now seems to have been exhausted and they are initiating proceedings against recalcitrant Member States: but they have effectively been pre-empted in this by the European Parliament.

So far as the "Thatcher Declaration" is concerned that presents no great problem. I think the Court would simply take the view that the measures taken by an individual Member State would need to be taken in the context of the abolition of the frontiers. In other words, the abolition of the frontiers would proceed and the Member States would be free to take whatever measures they thought necessary in the context of a Europe without internal frontiers. Because there has been so much misrepresentation of the Commission's proposals on the abolition of the internal frontiers, much of it emanating from unattributable briefing from "sources close to the British Government", perhaps I should explain just what it is the Commission proposed. We never at any time contemplated that the internal frontiers should be "no go" areas for the enforcement authorities. If there was good reason to suspect an individual or a consignment of goods of course it could be stopped whether at a frontier or anywhere else. The example I always gave was this: Piccadilly Circus is a well known haunt of drug pushers, and of course the police are entitled to pick up suspicious characters in the Circus or elsewhere: but imagine what an outcry there would be if the police erected barricades across Regent Street, Piccadilly and the Haymarket and stopped every vehicle and every pedestrian to check whether they were carrying drugs.

In fact it is well known, despite the government being reluctant to give full information, that most seizures are not made at the authorised entry points at the frontiers and in the minority of cases where they are it is usually the result of information received. The way one deals with these problems is not by wasting a large amount of manpower on ineffective controls, but by increased intelligence and heightened co-operation between the enforcement authorities of the Member States: and above all by strengthening the external frontiers to ensure that the evil does not penetrate into the Community in the first place.

But despite this rhetoric and vigorous defence of frontier controls, the British Government do seem to have recognised the realities of the situation and much has been done to relax controls for the ordinary traveller. But most of the Member States have moved further. The nine signatories of the Schengen Agreement – that is all the Member States other than the United Kingdom, Denmark and Greece – are now on course for total abolition of internal frontier controls on the free movement of people. While the date fixed has slipped more than once – primarily due to difficulties surrounding the creation of a computer operated system for the exchange of information – hopefully the Schengen Agreement will come into force in the course of 1994.

The Single Act contained another important provision. I decided early on that we should publish an Annual Progress Report. This was partly because of the interest shown by the European Parliament in the Internal Market Programme and the constant demand for information about progress. But also because I felt it essential to create a firm discipline to ensure that progress was indeed being made. The Annual Progress Report was designed specifically to show what delays had occurred and who was responsible for them: whether it was the Commission for failing to produce proposals on time: or the Parliament for not giving its opinion: or the Council for not getting on with the job. It proved also to be an invaluable tool inside the Commission Services themselves: because it meant that everyone knew precisely what was expected of them and that they would have to face public exposure of any shortcomings. It was also my own weapon in keeping my colleagues in the Commission up to scratch. But above all it was essential in dealing with the Council of Ministers who too often showed greater powers of disputation than ability to get on with the job.

The Single Act then greatly reinforced this discipline by providing that a Progress Report should be made to the Heads of Government at the halfway stage – that is before the end of 1988. This was not intended simply to give the

Heads of Government some interesting bedtime reading but to enable them to monitor progress and to take action where necessary.

This "half time" Report was then to be followed by a further Progress Report at the end of 1990 and a Final Report before the end of 1992. This Final Report was no longer to be simply a "Progress Report". The Commission was required to:

> "draw up an inventory of national laws, regulations and administrative provisions which fall under Article 100A [the Internal Market] and which have not been harmonised pursuant to that Article."

The provision then went on to say:

> "The Council [acting by majority voting] may decide that the provisions in force in a Member State must be recognised as being equivalent to those applied by another Member State."

In short, the intention was that after 1992 on matters affecting the Single Market there was to be mutual recognition of matters not yet harmonised. Unfortunately, the provision was not as strong as we in the Commission would have wanted. While "recognition" is governed by "must", "decision" is only governed by "may".

There is one other important aspect of the Single European Act which deserves mention.

Originally the European Parliament was simply a consultative body whose opinion was sought but as often as not ignored. Its only real powers were in the budgetary field but even those powers were limited. Its members were not directly elected but appointed by the Member States from their own Parliaments.

Over the years, the European Parliament, like all Parliaments, gradually extended its powers as often as not by procedural devices: and its claim to do so in the name of the people, as opposed to the governments, was greatly strengthened by the introduction in 1979 of direct elections. Now for the first time the Single European Act conferred on the European Parliament greatly increased powers principally in Internal Market matters through the so-called "co-operation procedure". Over the years the practice had grown up in the Parliament not of simply giving an "opinion" on a Commission proposal but of making very detailed amendments, sometimes extending the scope of the proposal and sometimes changing the very nature of the proposal. It would then try and put pressure on the Commission to accept its amendments by withholding, or threatening to withhold its "opinion" unless its demands were met. The Single Act, for the first time, gave legal backing to this direct involvement of the European Parliament in the legislative process principally in Internal Market matters. The "co-operation procedure" thus established was, on the surface at any rate, a procedure designed to secure agreement between the Parliament and the Council. In fact, it conferred a crucial role on the Commission who had to act as a mediator between the two bodies. The Commission tended very much to find itsclf on the same side as the Parliament. Both shared a commitment to a united Europe in contrast with the Council of Ministers which tended very much to protect the narrower "national" interest. The Parliament, however, greatly resented what they felt to be grossly inadequate powers conferred upon them by the Single Act. There were threats to invoke the "Doomsday" powers invested in the Parliament by Article 146 of the Treaty to dismiss the Commission and these threats were repeated in the context of demanding that the Commission support all amendments passed by the Parliament irrespective of the merits or of the Commission's own views. It was, of course, all nonsense. The Parliament's real enemy was the Council: the Commission tended very much to be the Parliament's ally: and to attack your ally in order to vent your spleen on your enemy is not on the whole a wise or productive procedure. In any event a "Doomsday" provision of the kind contained in Article 146 is of very little practical use. It is something like the nuclear bomb: it never has been used: is unlikely to be used: and if it were used the outcome would be impossible to predict, except that it would probably be disastrous not least to those instigating it as indeed happened when Samson pulled down the pillars of the Temple. In the event, the co-operation procedure proved to be a great success: it enabled the Parliament to exercise a considerable influence on Internal Market matters: the great majority of its amendments were in fact adopted: and I myself found the support of the Parliament extremely valuable. But the question of the Parliament's powers has not gone away: and it has been one of the major issues in the Maastricht Treaty. The outcome, predictable enough, was that the Parliament acquired some, but very limited, increase in its powers; it succeeded in getting some control over the Commission and the appointment of its President and members; and a pourboire was thrown in in the form of an agreement that the Institutional Question (as it is known) should be an important part of the grand review which the Treaty provided should take place in 1996.

The Single Act was negotiated at Luxembourg in December 1985: the drafting was completed in the next few weeks and the Act was signed in February 1986. It was intended that after ratification by the national Parliaments it would come into force on 1 January 1987. But the Irish Government ran into trouble with its Constitution. A referendum to amend the Constitution was required: that was successfully accomplished, the Treaty was duly ratified and came into force on 1 July 1987, six months late. Years later the Maastricht Treaty was to run into similar but more serious troubles.

Despite the delay in ratification due to the Irish problem a decision was taken by the Council of Ministers immediately the Act was signed that they would act as though the Act was in force and in particular to proceed by majority voting on Internal Market matters, using if necessary the device of abstention to avoid conflict on matters still technically requiring unanimity.

Finally, one comment. The success of the Single Act was itself a reflection of the success of the Internal Market Programme and of the Single Market it created and it is in this sense that I have described the Internal Market Programme as "the Flagship of the Enterprise". Interestingly, this verdict is confirmed by Emanuele Gazzo, the Editor of *Agence Europe* and the spiritual heir of Altieri Spinelli. In the issue of *Agence Europe* of 25 April 1991 he wrote:

> "We are told: 'remember the Single Act: people ranted and raved about it and it ended up a success'. The argument is flawed. Because it is not the Single Act that was successful, but the credibility it attributed (via certain of its provisions) to the realization, within a certain time limit, of the Single Market, an objective that stirred opinion."

## Chapter 6
# Implementing the Single Market Programme

## Success achieved

In looking at the measures taken to ensure the implementation of the White Paper Programme it is necessary to describe briefly the legislation process in the Community. Legislation may be in the form of a Regulation, a Directive, or a Decision. The commonest form of all is a Directive which in effect "directs" the Member States to legislate (or take other effective legal action) on the basis set out in the Directive. A Directive tends now to be in great detail, very much like an Act of Parliament: but it does leave Member States with some discretion just how they will draft their own domestic legislation. A Regulation in contrast has direct effect: it does not need translation into national law. As a result it has to be drafted with the detail and precision one would find in a Statute. Customs Union matters are nearly always dealt with by Regulation. The customs duties are Community resources and external trade matters fall within Community, not national, competence. The customs services in the individual Member States operate on behalf of the Community. Viewed against this background uniformity of administration and law is essential. This means that the actual operative legislation must be Community legislation and that means a Regulation as opposed to a Directive. In recent years in other areas there has been a move away from Directives to Regulations. The Treaty also provides that, in certain instances, matters may be dealt with by a Council "Decision" which has direct legislative effect. In some areas the Commission also has power to make "Decisions". "Decisions" of this kind, which frequently relate to specific circumstances or matters, *e.g.* agricultural prices or competition matters, are of little importance in relation to the White Paper Programme.

Under the terms of the Treaty all legislation must start with a "proposal" from the Commission which has the sole right of initiative. Of course the Commission does not act in a vacuum. If the Heads of Government meeting in the European Council ask for measures to be taken, the Commission will usually respond. So too if the Parliament presses for legislation, the Commission will if it thinks it necessary and practicable table the legislation asked for: but here the Commission has to take account of the fact that there would be little point in tabling legislation which it knew would be blocked by the Council of Ministers. Despite intense pressure, none of this has been changed by the Maastricht Treaty in areas of Community competence.

The Commission's "proposal" in the form of a draft Directive or Regulation will normally be drawn up after consultation, sometimes extensive, with interested parties. When the draft is settled and approved by the full Commission it then goes simultaneously to the Council and the Parliament, and often to the Economic and Social Committee as well. This is not the end, indeed it is only the beginning, of the Commission's involvement as it now has the task of steering the draft proposal through both the

Council and the Parliament and consulting with the Economic and Social Committee where the Treaty so provides. The process is not unlike taking legislation through the Westminster Parliament. Extensive amendment may be needed, and usually is, to meet the concerns of the individual Member States who form the Council of Ministers, and of the Parliament. Hopefully the draft will complete the course successfully and the Directive or Regulation will be adopted. It will then be the responsibility of the individual Member States in the case of a Directive to transpose it into national law. Progress in the past had often been excruciatingly slow. Almost the first two Directives which I successfully piloted through the Council are typical examples: that on architects had taken 17 years and that on pharmacists 16 years. Some Directives remained permanently blocked. Just occasionally the blockage would be due to irreconcilable differences between the Parliament and the Council, the Council being unwilling to assert its final authority.

So far as the Commission itself was concerned, progress was primarily a matter under our own control, although the perennial shortage of staff was a constant problem. Contrary to the views propagated in the United Kingdom, the total staff of the Commission is very small, much smaller than that of the average government Department and although there are areas of inefficiency they are no more significant than those in the UK's own bureaucracy and the claims of excessively detailed legislation "imposed" by Brussels have now been exposed as largely the handiwork of government Departments at home. I had secured control of virtually all the Services which were directly involved in the Internal Market Programme and this greatly simplified both co-ordination and control. But arrangements were also set in place to secure proper co-ordination across the whole field and to monitor and ensure progress in areas for which other Commissioners were responsible. This general oversight and control of the programme was vested in DGIII with Fernand Braun as the Director General and Riccardo Perissich as the Deputy Director General with specific responsibility for the programme. These arrangements worked efficiently and well and great credit for the success of the programme must go to Fernand and Riccardo. Fernand Braun has now retired: his place as Director General has been taken by Riccardo Perissich. No better appointment could have been made.

While we could in the Commission organise our own work in this way, the work of the Council was the Council's responsibility although the Commission inevitably played a prominent, and at times dominant, role in the Council's operations. The new procedures, and particularly majority voting, prescribed by the Single Act were critically important. But much needed to be done in addition to improve the way the Council itself handled its work.

Each Member State holds the Presidency of the Council for six months. Hitherto each successive Presidency had drawn up its own six month programme reflecting its own view of "priorities" or measures in which it had a particular interest. But six months is too short a time to push a measure through from inception to adoption: and all too often the next Presidency would have a different set of priorities and it would leave the measures started, but unfinished, by its predecessor on one side. The result was a plethora of half finished proposals and very little progress. Clearly this would not do if the White Paper Programme was to be carried through successfully and on time. The issue was taken up immediately by Luxembourg which assumed the Presidency of the Council within a matter of days after the Heads of Government had endorsed the White Paper Programme. A "Troika" system was set up under which in future a rolling programme should be adopted as agreed between the retiring Presidency, the incoming Presidency and the one following. This programme should specify the subjects to be tackled and the measures to be adopted in the following 12 months, *i.e.* the incoming Presidency and the one after that. On this basis, the Luxembourg, Netherlands and UK Presidencies agreed a programme which envisaged the adoption of 100 of the measures set out in the White Paper during 1986.

Underlying the detailed planning in the White Paper was the realization that if the programme was to be completed and in force by the end of 1992 adequate time had to be provided both for the Council to consider the individual proposals in detail and for their incorporation into domestic, *i.e.* national, law. Broadly speaking, we assumed that the Council needed on average two years to adopt a proposal and that it would take a further two years to incorporate proposals once adopted into national law. This meant that the programme had to be very heavily "front end" loaded. Thus, broadly speaking, the Commission would need to produce – or "table" as it is commonly called – virtually all the 300 proposals in the White Paper by the end of 1988. The Council in turn would need to adopt all the proposals by the end of 1990 and the Parliament in its turn would need to complete its own work in time for the Council to achieve this deadline. The approach adopted in the programme meant that the work of the Commission would be exceptionally heavy in the first four years – that is until the end of 1988 – as it would have to cope both with producing the proposals and piloting them through the Council and the Parliament. But thereafter its work on the programme would tail off. Correspondingly, if the programme was strictly adhered to, the Council's work would be completed by the end of 1990. In this sense, a considerable safety margin was quite deliberately built into the programme. I never disclosed this as I was certain the safety margin would be needed: but if the others involved ever discovered that within reason slippage could be accommodated, the slippage would occur whether justified or not and we might well end up by missing the 1992 deadline. There was another factor also which I will deal with in more detail later. As the structure of the Single Act itself indicated, the Internal Market Programme was the first step in a process which was designed to lead to European Union. The momentum once generated by the White Paper Programme must not be lost. This meant that well before 1992 the planning and preparatory work for the next step towards European Union must be put in hand: and this in turn meant that both energy and resources must be left available. In short, as the pressure of work on the White Paper Programme eased off, slack became available to set in train the next step to European Union. And so indeed it proved.

When one comes to look at the progress which was in fact achieved, the first point to make is that neither Commission nor Council started from scratch. Of the 300 White Paper proposals, approximately 100 had already been tabled – *i.e.* were already in the hands of both Council and Parliament – at the time the White Paper Programme was launched. But it would be quite wrong to draw the conclusion that in fact there were really only 200 and not 300 proposals to be dealt with. Unfortunately most of the proposals on the table were difficult and contentious and many of them had been bogged down in the

Council for years. They were therefore to require a great deal of additional work both by the Commission and the Council. Indeed in retrospect I wish that we could have started with a completely clean sheet instead of having to take over a corpus of old proposals which not only required refurbishing but many of which had accumulated deeply ingrained prejudices and entrenched positions.

On a single arithmetical basis the Commission would need to produce 50 new proposals (draft Directives or Regulations) each year over the years 1985 to 1988 inclusive, while the Council would need to adopt also 50 measures a year but over the extended period 1985 to 1990 inclusive. The actual planning was rather more sophisticated than this. As the first Progress Report indicates, the programme envisaged that 48 new proposals should have been tabled by the Commission in 1985 plus the first three months of 1986 (in addition to the 100 already on the table) and a further 50 proposals in the remainder of 1986. So far as the Council was concerned, the programme envisaged that 61 proposals would be adopted in 1985 and a further 71 in 1986. The fact that the programme envisaged the Council adopting a greater number of proposals in the first two years (1985 and 1986) than the Commission would table simply reflects the fact already mentioned that the Council started with a stock of approximately 100 proposals which had already been tabled at the time the White Paper was published.

In the early days performance fell far short of target. Up to 31 March 1986 the Commission tabled only 28 new proposals against the 48 envisaged in the programme while the Council had adopted only 27 against the 61 envisaged. But as time went on the slippage was retrieved. Incidentally, there is always a slight problem in compiling figures of this sort: for example, a document may for various reasons bear a date a few days or even a few weeks later than it was actually adopted.

In the second Progress Report, dated May 1987 but with the figures made up to 31 March 1987, the Commission was shown as having virtually caught up with 175 proposals in all, having been presented out of a total now reduced to 287. The Council still lagged behind having achieved a total of 58 only. In the Council's defence two points need to be made. First, the Single Act with its majority voting procedure for Internal Market matters did not come into force until 1 July 1987, although the Member States had agreed, informally, that they would respect its provisions without awaiting the formal date. Secondly, the Council is "at the end of the line", both Commission and Parliament having to complete their procedures before the Council can formally decide, or even start work. By the time the third Report was presented in March 1988, the Commission had presented in all 208 proposals out of a total, now, of about 280: the Council had adopted 69, plus a further six partially adopted, and a "common position" that is, political agreement on the part of the Council, having been reached in another 14 cases. The biggest area of delay throughout, both on the part of the Commission and the Council, was in the area of agriculture. This reflected the fact that both the Commission Services involved (DGVI) and the Council of Agricultural Ministers attached a higher priority to setting farm prices than to the White Paper Programme. The Common Agricultural Policy has always been an albatross around the Community's neck.

At the Commission's last meeting before the Summer Recess in 1987, I was asked by Jacques Delors what message I would wish to give to my colleagues before they departed for their summer holidays. I said we had now less than 18 months to go before our own term of office came to an end (technically on 5 January 1989 although most people would think the date was 31 December 1988): it was essential that before we left office progress on the Internal Market Programme should be such that it was "irreversible" so that our successors would have to complete the job with no excuse for backsliding or having their attention diverted to other matters. I reminded the Commission that this was the goal I had set, and indeed in these very words, when I had first talked to them about the programme, right back in January 1985. If we were to achieve that target, then the Commission ought to present all of its proposals by the end of 1988, although I would accept 90%: the Council in its turn must adopt half or 50%. It was useless waiting until the autumn of next year (1988), when we were due to present the "half time" Report to the Heads of Government required under the specific terms of the Single European Act, before we took action, or more likely panicked.

In the months that followed there was a sharp acceleration in the completion of the work. To such an extent that the Heads of Government meeting at Hannover in June 1988 were able to declare that progress was such that the programme was now "irreversible" – "a fact" they said "recognised by those engaged in economic and social life". By the year end when my own term of office came to an end, the Commission had in fact achieved its target of 90%: the Council, as I had expected, fell somewhat short of its target of 50% although if common positions were counted, the shortfall was marginal.

Another four years was to elapse before 31 December 1992, four years dominated by other matters and in particular the Maastricht Treaty and all the troubles it involved. Nevertheless the Internal Market Programme forged ahead. When Jacques Delors came to talk to the European Parliament in March 1991, he reported that the Commission had for all practical purposes presented virtually every single one of the proposals contained in the White Paper and the Council had at last passed the 200 mark; and he urged the Council to complete their task by the end of the year to leave the Member States sufficient time to pass the necessary legislation in time for the proposals to come into force by 31 December 1992.

It is always difficult to give a final score: some of the original proposals in the White Paper will have been dropped: some will have been adopted in part only: some will have been divided: some proposals will have been added and it can be a moot point whether those added are real additions or in substitution for proposals originally included or in elaboration of those proposals. But the Report to the UK Parliament on "Developments in the European Community January to June 1993" gives a figure of 264 proposals adopted out of a revised total of 282 and it says:

> "The Single Market was declared complete in all essential respects by the Edinburgh Council in December 1992."

and it refers only to the need for:

> "a certain amount of residual legislative activity in order to complete the Single Market in detailed respects and in order to update existing legislation."

The one significant area in which performance fell significantly short of target, namely the freedom of movement of persons, is not mentioned. But subject to this, I think it is a fair verdict to say that so far as the institutions of the Community were concerned, they had fully met their obligations to ensure that the deadline of 31 December 1992 for the completion of the Internal Market Programme was met.

But considerable delay remained regarding the incorporation, or "transposition" as it is technically known, of the Community law into national law. Some Member States, notably Denmark and the United Kingdom had done particularly well; others, notably Italy, had fallen badly behind. The difference often depended upon Parliamentary procedure rather than on any question of goodwill or deliberate delay. The issue is of course critically important. At the end of the day what matters is not simply that the rules of the integrated Single Market should be agreed at Community level, but that they should take effect on the ground. The Commission with the support of the Heads of Government exerted considerable pressure, opening proceedings in the Court of Justice against Member States in breach of their obligations where this became necessary. While not entirely satisfactory, the position is now greatly improved with countries like Denmark, the United Kingdom and now Italy with 90% or more of measures requiring transposition having been so transposed.

The Court of Justice has also played a significant part. In a scrics of judgments the Court has held that if the terms of a Directive are sufficiently clear and specific the Directive can be enforced once its application date has been reached even if the national legislation required has not been adopted.

I pass from this general review to make a brief comment on the role of the United Kingdom when it occupied the Presidency.

The United Kingdom was indeed to occupy the Presidency in the six months to 31 December 1992 which saw the successful completion of the Single Market

Programme. But it had also held the Presidency in the second half of 1986 while I was in the Commission and the programme was then in the early stages of implementation. This was a crucially important period as success in the early days would be vital in giving validity and authority to the programme and could well determine its success or failure.

The UK Presidency in 1986 was a period of sunshine and showers and it ended with one almighty storm.

Early in the Presidency I was given the most welcome task of extending to the members of the Commission and their wives an invitation from Her Majesty to attend one of her Garden Parties in Buckingham Palace.

Jacques Delors introduced everybody to the Queen: I to the Duke of Edinburgh. In the evening through the kindness of Geoffrey Howe my wife and I hosted a reception at Admiralty House.

From the point of view of the Commission, therefore, the Presidency had started on a particularly enjoyable note. But in terms of completion of work, November arrived and very little hard progress had been made. At this point the Prime Minister decided to take a personal hand in the conduct of affairs. She wrote to every Head of Government telling them that it simply was not good enough and she proposed sending a team of Ministers around the capitals of Europe to settle with the individual Ministers responsible for the differences which had held up progress. The tactic was entirely successful and produced what was by far and away the best result that any Presidency had so far achieved. And it set the pattern for the future. This was the Prime Minister at her ablest and best.

The storm, however, was soon to break. The Summit – that is the meeting of the Heads of Government – was held in London on 5 and 6 December (1986). At the end of the Conference the Head of Government of the host Member State holds a press conference accompanied by the President of the Commission. The Prime Minister conducted affairs in her usual rumbustious style completely oblivious to the presence of Jacques Delors who was getting more and more frustrated or outraged. Realising her mistake she turned to him in a grievously mistaken air of jocularity and demanded whether he had anything to say. Jacques Delors remained silent. But he had not forgotten: still less forgiven.

Shortly afterwards on 9 December and strictly following convention, the Prime Minister went to Strasbourg to address the European Parliament. Her speech contained some pretty strong and provocative comments. Jacques Delors, who was reporting to the Parliament on behalf of the Commission, made a robust reply highly critical of the attitude of the United Kingdom. As a result of the exchanges both felt hurt and outraged. Jacques Delors initially refused to attend the ceremonial lunch. I unfortunately found myself in the company of the Prime Minister. "The bloody man", she kept declaiming in a stage whisper which could be heard far beyond the boundaries of the great hall, "I gave him every chance to speak at the press conference in London and he wouldn't say a word. Now he takes this opportunity to attack me hoping I won't be able to answer back". In the end peace was restored and Jacques Delors was induced to come to lunch. But I doubt whether he has ever forgotten.

There is one further matter which deserves mention. Shortly after the publication of the White Paper and in the light of widespread concern expressed that the effect might be to favour the prosperous North and prejudice the struggling and poorer economies of the South, Jacques Delors asked Tommaso Padoa-Schioppa to report on the likely effect of the programme on regional disparities. Mr Padoa-Schioppa was Deputy Governor of the Bank of Italy but he had also been Dircctor General of DGII in the Commission Services, DGII being responsible for Economic and Monetary matters. The Padoa-Schioppa report was of enormous interest: but unfortunately, from my point of view at any rate, it concentrated unduly on monetary matters and left largely unanswered the impact of the programme on regional economic differences.

Shortly afterwards, early in 1986, I commissioned Paolo Cecchini, who had just retired as Deputy Director General of DGIII and was a man of immense knowledge and experience and well regarded throughout the Community, to conduct a major study into the benefits of the 1992 Programme for the Community as a whole. Interestingly, hitherto the issues involved had always been addressed under the head of the "Costs of non-Europe". I was determined to break away from this negative approach and turn our attention positively to the *benefits* of creating a Single Market. The Cecchini study was one of the most ambitious pieces of market research ever undertaken. In addition to the Commission Services, 15 firms of consultants were involved, university departments, distinguished academics, leaders of industry and most significant of all 11,000 enterprises which co-operated in the enquiry. The Report was published in 1988. The popular version, which was translated into all of the Community languages and has also appeared in Japanese, is entitled "The European challenge 1992: the benefits of a Single Market". It runs to 106 pages. The full report, which is a mine of detailed information about individual countries and individual industries, runs to something like 6,000 pages. For anyone seriously interested in the economic future of Europe, its present shortfalls and its potential benefits, it was compul-

Members of the new European Commission at the Abbey of Royaumont, near Paris, December 1984. From left to right: Willy de Clerck, Alois Pfeiffer, Peter Sutherland, Nic Mosar, Henning Christophersen, Frans Andriessen, Carlo Ripa di Meana, President Jacques Delors, Karl-Heinz Narjes, Lord Cockfield, Stanley Clinton-Davis, Lorenzo Natali, Grigoris Varfis.

© Directorate General for Information of the Commission of the European Communities

The author (right) with Jacques Delors.
© Directorate General for Information of the Commission of the European Communities

The author (while Minister of State at the Treasury) with George Bush (left) and Lord Weinstock (right).
© The White House

The Prince of Wales with the author on his official visit to the Commission in March 1987.

© Directorate General for Information of the Commission of the European Communities

sive – rather than just compulsory – reading. I would only hope that at some time we will have a new version of Cecchini showing what has been done, what has been achieved and what remains to be done – a "Cecchini Revisited".

A comment too on what might be described as "Public Awareness". I take as my examples France and the Great Paris Conference: and the United Kingdom and the Lancaster House Conference.

## The Great Paris Conference

On 5 and 6 of December 1987 an event occurred in Paris which did more than anything to propel the bandwagon along the road. A gigantic Conference under the slogan "Europe 1992" was organised by Giscard d'Estaing, former President of France, supported by James Callaghan, former Prime Minister of Great Britain, and Helmut Schmidt, former Federal Chancellor of Germany. The Conference was attended by Jacques Delors and myself as representing the Commission, by Ministers and former Ministers from the Community countries, by ex-Presidents of the Commission and former Commissioners, by leaders of trade and industry throughout Europe, by distinguished academics, by newspaper correspondents from Europe, America and the Far East and above all by 4,000 of the citizens of Europe. The event was held in the Great Hall of UNESCO and it was televised live throughout the whole of Europe and places beyond. Giscard d'Estaing had his own television crew and a man with a TV camera was crawling around our feet all the time so that throughout the Conference pictures were projeted of Giscard d'Estaing speaking: or Giscard d'Estaing listening:

or Giscard d'Estaing agreeing: or at times even disagreeing.

It was one of the most dramatic events I have ever attended. And when you consider it was held on a Saturday and Sunday when the 4,000 people who attended came in their own time and not in their employers' time, the enthusiasm generated in France by the 1992 Programme could be both seen and believed.

There was one incident that has remained firmly in my mind. I was sitting on the platform with Giscard d'Estaing and the Moderator of an open discussion. The task of the Moderator is to keep the discussion lively, to pick those wanting to speak and even to provoke those who might have a contribution to make to do so. Spying David Steel, the then leader of the British Liberal Party, in the audience, she called upon him to speak. He declined. It must be the first time in human history that a leading politician has refused to talk live before an audience of 320 million people. The Moderator, taken aback, exclaimed:

"I had hoped we would have heard an English voice in our discussions."

Up leapt Giscard d'Estaing. "But we have", he said, "Lord Cockfield is sitting by me and we have heard from him twice". To me the most touching part of this exchange was that I could speak not once but twice and no one realised that I was British and not just a European.

## The Lancaster House Conference

The Lancaster House Conference is a rather sad epilogue to this story of the way that the 1992 Programme fired the imagination of the people rather than just the politicians. At the Conservative Party Conference in October 1987, David Young, then Secretary of State for Trade and Industry, announced that he would be launching a major campaign to arouse awareness of the 1992 Programme in trade and industry and a great Conference would be held at Lancaster House the following May, a date subsequently brought forward to April. This peculiar sense of urgency – a date nearly three years after the White Paper had been published and six months after the announcement – meant that this "great initiative" petered out into the sand. I was asked to make a video tape as an introduction which I did. The Prime Minister opened the Conference. I was not invited. I don't know how many people came. All in all it was a sad occasion: sad for me, sad for my country.

## The Single Market Programme and its place in history

Whatever now happens, the completion of the Internal Market Programme and its completion on time is an achievement without parallel in the history of the Community. It had none of the advantages of enthusiasm and euphoria which attended the launch of the Community in 1957 and saw it through its first momentous ten years of life. On the contrary it had to face disillusion, defeatism and obstruction, the legacy of ten years or more of stagnation and narrow nationalism. The sheer breadth and depth of the programme, the way that it permeated every aspect of European life meant that the work involved was daunting both in magnitude and complexity. It meant resolving differences of opinion and approach of 12 very diverse Member States compared with the six, relatively compatible, members of the Community when it was first founded. It had to tackle and solve problems which had grown in complexity and controversy because they had remained unsolved for so long. None of this could have been tackled and tackled successfully without a new spirit in the Community, in the Commission and in the Services. Perhaps the greatest achievement of the programme was that it called forth this new spirit. When the history of our times comes to be written, I am sure that it will be this which will be regarded as marking the turning point in the fortunes of the Community. What we really succeeded in doing was to prove that if you can move one mountain, then you can move other mountains too.

# Chapter 7
# The Institutions of the Community

There is a striking similarity between the institutional framework of the European Community and that of the United States of America. Both have a separate and independent executive, a separate and independent legislature and a separate and independent judiciary. The similarity is not accidental or purely a matter of coincidence. Neither is derived from the other. But both share a common philosophical parentage. The American Constitution was based upon the theories of the French political philosopher, the Count de Montesquieu, and particularly upon his Theory of the Separation of Powers. That theory in turn was based on his understanding of the British Constitution. Some people would say "his misunderstanding" of the British Constitution, a simple enough error as the British Constitution is unwritten. But I think the better analysis is that it is the British Constitution itself, and primarily because it is unwritten, which has strayed from its 18th century pattern. The European Community is essentially a French creation: its philosophical foundation is French: and to this day the working language of the Community is French. It is not surprising therefore that its institutional framework should reflect French political philosophy and particularly Montesquieu's Theory of the

Separation of Powers. When Mrs Thatcher denounced Jacques Delors' restatement – because it was no more than a restatement – of the basic institutional framework of the Community with her emphatic "No, No, No", she did so from a profound misunderstanding of the Community, its origins and its political philosophy.

The Commission is the executive arm of the Community: the Parliament and the Council of Ministers share the legislative function: and the Court of Justice in Luxembourg is the judiciary. But before I deal with them in detail it is necessary to make this point about the way the British Constitution itself has developed. In the 17th century there was a clear separation between the executive arm of government, which consisted of the King and his Ministers, and the Parliament, which after the Civil War and most certainly after the Bill of Rights, assumed virtually unchallenged legislative power, that retained by the King being minimal. But with the accession of the Hanoverians – "German George" could not even speak English – Parliament and particularly its leaders effectively assumed also the executive function. The Cabinet and particularly its leader the Prime Minister were *de facto*, but not *de jure*, drawn from one or other House of Parliament. But in the present century the tables have effectively been turned. The executive – no longer the King but now the Prime Minister and his (or her) government – have assumed control over the legislature by means of the Party system, "whipping", the selection of candidates by small party caucuses, the need for their approval by Party hierarchies, "deselection" and so forth. Even the date of the General Election is controlled in very large measure by the government which is not above using the threat of a General Election, and the potential loss of their seats, to keep recalcitrant members of Parliament in line. And now of course the Members of the House of Lords are largely appointed by the government *i.e.* the executive; and if hereditary Peers were barred, as some would want, the House of Lords would become entirely appointed by the executive.

Very occasionally the legislature, in the true sense of the term, revolts and the Prime Minister and his (or her) government are thrown out. But it is an interesting example of how far the British Constitution has departed from principle that Mrs Thatcher was ejected not by the electorate, not by Parliament acting in its true capacity as the legislature, but by a Party caucus with neither legal nor constitutional standing. Moreover the Party caucus was acting not from any motive of public interest but because the polls showed that with Mrs Thatcher as leader, the Party had no chance of winning the next General Election and this would mean the loss of their own seats. In other words, they behaved no differently from the passengers on the sinking ship who rush for the lifeboats. Mrs Thatcher herself is now expressing great indignation about the way she was displaced. She was of course entirely right. But what happened on that occasion is ultimately a reflection of the peculiarities of the British Constitution which she was always at great pains to defend and from which herself – and her Party – had greatly benefited.

So I now turn to the individual institutions. So far as the Court of Justice is concerned, it retains its complete independence. I do not therefore comment on it except in so far as its judgments are relevant in relation to institutional matters. But the other three institutions, namely the Commission, the Parliament and the Council of Ministers, I now deal with individually and in detail. Under the terms of the Maastricht Treaty, the Court of Auditors has been promoted to the status of an "institution" of the

Community. But as the present treatise does not deal with the Maastricht Treaty except *en passant*, I leave the Court of Auditors on one side.

# The Commission – the executive arm of the Community

The Commission has three principal functions: the right of initiative: its duty as "guardian of the Treaties": and thirdly the day to day management of the Community.

## The right of initiative

Under the terms of the Treaty the Commission has "the right of initiative", indeed the sole right of initiative. In other words, the sole right of initiating legislation rests with the Commission. The reason is quite simple: if all 12 Member States plus the Parliament were all allowed to institute legislation, the result would be total confusion with everyone proposing what suited them with scant regard to what suited others or the Community as a whole. The Commission is regarded as representing the Community interest: and it follows logically that the Commission should take the initiative. This does not mean that the Commission is not responsive to the wishes of the Council, or the Member States that compose it, or of the Parliament. But its ultimate right of initiative is a jealously guarded function. Both the Council and the Parliament have tried to encroach upon it: but so far without success. The Parliament, while I was in the Commission, tried to promote "own initiative" legislation but the Commission faced them down although it was left to me to do that unpopular duty. Unfortunately, Jacques Delors, himself a former Member of the European Parliament, was tempted at times to make speeches in the European Parliament, entirely from the best motives, but which fuelled their ambition. They thought the door had been opened. It had not and I had to shut it. Fortunately, the Parliament made the mistake of promoting a piece of patently unnecessary legislation, arguing that what they wanted to do was to establish the "principle". But anyone who tries to build "principle" on the sand of unnecessary legislation deserves the fate likely to overcome him. But the issue has not and will not go away despite the failure of the Maastricht Treaty to confer additional powers on the Parliament in this respect. But before anyone in this country gets too indignant in supporting the Parliament's claim, it would be as well to remember how brutal the government, *i.e.* the executive, is in this country in restricting the right of Private Members, the remaining vestige of an independent legislature, to introduce and enact legislation that they, rather than the executive, favour.

There is an interesting tactic employed by the Commission in this area which I greatly developed as part of the underpinning of the Internal Market Programme. Although it was entirely a matter for the Commission to decide what legislation to propose, nevertheless, we prompted the Heads of Government meeting in the European Council to ask the Commission to produce the legislation needed either generally or on particular subjects. An early and important example of this tactic is to be seen in the way the White Paper Programme for the Completion of the Internal Market was launched. As I have already described, I had agreed the basis on which the programme should be drawn up before I even came to the Commission and I had received the Commission's endorsement in our very early days. This was followed up by the Commission presenting its Work Programme for 1985 to the European Parliament on 6 March of that year. The Work Programme contained the following statement:

> "The Commission will be asking the European Council to pledge itself to completion of a fully unified internal market by 1992 and to approve the necessary programme together with a realistic and binding timetable."

The European Council duly obliged and the Conclusions of the Summit held at Brussels on 29 and 30 March 1985 read as follows:

> "The European Council laid particular emphasis on . . . action to achieve a single large market by 1992 . . . it called upon the Commission to draw up a detailed programme with a specific timetable before its next meeting."

A casual or incomplete reading of the documents might have suggested that the initiative had come from the European Council. But as the full record shows, the initiative had in fact come from the Commission, in the exercise of its sole right of initiative, and the European Council was responding to that initiative. But the public endorsement by the European Council on this and indeed on subsequent occasions was not only valuable in public relations terms but of the utmost value in dealing with the Council of Ministers. It enabled me in particular to argue that the principle had already been decided by their Heads of Government and their concern was not to debate the principle but to deal with the legislation which implemented the principle. It may be thought to be a diversion from my main theme to deal with a matter of this kind, but I fear that unless I record it no one will, nor is it the kind of point an outside observer is likely to know.

# The Commission as the "guardian of the Treaties"

The second of the Commission's functions is to act as the "guardian of the Treaties", a role conferred on it by Article 155 of the Treaty although the term itself was coined by the Court of Justice. Here the Commission's duty is not exclusive: in certain areas, particularly where the Commission fails to act, the Council or the Parliament, a Member State, or even an individual who is aggrieved can take proceedings and sometimes they do. But the primary responsibility rests upon the Commission. Thus, it is the Commission's duty to ensure that Directives are incorporated into domestic, *i.e.* national, law and correctly incorporated. A "Directive" is so called because it is a "directive" to Member States to legislate, or take other effective action, to implement the provisions set out in the Directive. A Regulation, in contrast, sets out the legislation in detail and it has direct effect without the need for national legislation. The Member States have always tended to favour the Directive as opposed to the Regulation as it gives them a greater degree of discretion in drafting their domestic legislation, sometimes genuinely in order to meet local peculiarities, sometimes with less merit to enable them surreptitiously to water down the Directive. As the years have gone by, Directives have gone into greater and greater detail and the stage has been reached where they often resemble detailed legislation. To some extent this reflects the increase in the size and diversity of the Community and the determination of disparate Member States to ensure that their particular needs or prejudices are amply covered. To some extent it reflects a determination to cut down the scope or effectiveness of the legislation by the introduction of all sorts of qualifications or exceptions. There is now a reaction to this. Thus, the President of the Court of Justice, Mr Ole Due, has advocated the use of Regulations rather than Directives, to avoid the need, with its consequential delay and uncertainty, of incorporating Community legislation into domestic law. In the opposite sense, one of the proposals before the Intergovernmental Conference on Political Union was that legislation should take two forms: "framework legislation" which would deal essentially with the principles and would go through the full proposed procedure with greatly increased participation by the Parliament; and "detailed legislation" giving effect to the "framework legislation" which would be the subject of a much simplified procedure. This proposal disappeared in the course of the negotiations but it may live to return another day.

It is the Commission's duty also to ensure that the provisions of the Treaty itself and of legislation under the Treaty once enacted are properly enforced. Some of the provisions of the Treaty are directly applicable. Perhaps the most important example is Article 30 which provides for the freedom of movement of goods: *prima facie* any obstacle to the freedom of movement of goods is unlawful and has to be justified – if it can be justified – under the terms of the Treaty, for example under Article 36 which sets out a long catalogue of exemptions from Article 30. This is an area which has been productive of a great deal of litigation. But other provisions of the Treaty are not directly applicable. They may, for example, provide specifically that Directives should be adopted to give effect to the provisions concerned. Or the Court may decide, as it did in the *Insurance Cases* in 1986, that the legitimate divergence of legislation in Member States was so great that a degree of harmonization was necessary before effect could be given to the provision of the Treaty providing for the freedom of movement of services. But there is an increasing tendency for the Court to hold that provisions of the Treaty *are* directly applicable. Thus, in the extremely important areas of competition, mergers and state aids the Commission can and does act directly by reference to the provisions of the Treaty without the need and largely in the absence of detailed legislation by way of Directive or Regulation. This does not mean that detailed legislation cannot be enacted. The recent Mergers Regulation is an example: but the real purpose of that legislation was not to enable the Commission to act, it had that power under the Treaty, but to give it virtually the *exclusive* right of action in a defined area.

The Internal Market Programme itself has greatly enhanced the importance of the Commission's enforcement activity. By the end of 1992 the legislation had virtually all been enacted at the Community level. But that legislation must, where needed, be incorporated – or "transposed" to use the technical term – into domestic legislation and if a Member State fails to transpose the legislation, or does so incorrectly, it is the Commission's duty to take action. So to, if the Member State fails to enforce the legislation, the duty to see that it is enforced rests fairly and squarely on the Commission's shoulders. But it is only fair to the Commission to make the point that it can only act if it receives the evidence needed: and that evidence must come either from other Member States or from aggrieved individuals or enterprises. There is therefore a burden of responsibility not only on Member States but also on trade and industry to ensure that the rules of the Single Market are respected.

## The day to day management of the Community

Thirdly, the Commission is responsible for the day to day management of the Community, in just the same way as a Minister in the United Kingdom and his Department are responsible for the day to day management of his area of activity. In some instances this is specifically set out in the Treaty. Thus in the case of the Common Agricultural Policy, Article 46 provides that it should be the Commission which fixes the level of import levies on agricultural products: and in the case of overseas trade, Article 113 provides that it should be the Commission which conducts negotiations with third countries. More generally, Article 145 provides that "in the acts the Council adopts" it should confer on the Commission "powers for the implementation of the rules which the Council lays down" although the Council retains the right if it so wishes to "exercise directly implementing powers itself". Article 155 is even wider in its scope. The article confers wide-ranging powers on the Commission "to ensure the proper functioning and development of the common market": and *inter alia* it provides for the Council to delegate to the Commission powers to implement policies or provisions which the Council has agreed.

This delegation of powers to the Commission often takes the form of setting up a Committee. This Committee can simply be an Advisory Committee in which event the decision remains firmly in the hands of the Commission although in practice the advice of the Committee is rarely disregarded. Or it can be a "Regulatory Committee", that is, it decides whether or not the Commission's proposed action should be accepted. In a Regulatory Committee, although in law a Commission Committee presided over by the Commission, only the representatives of the Member States can vote and increasingly over the years the

Member States succeeded in transferring what were intended to be powers of implementation vested in the Commission back to themselves. The result more often than not was paralysis as the Member States simply could not decide among themselves. The Single European Act set out to reverse this process and in a Declaration appended to the Act the Member States said that in matters affecting the Internal Market preference was to be given to the Advisory Committee procedure, which meant that the Committee could "advise" but it was the Commission which decided. The Declaration was very strongly worded and it is therefore worth quoting:

> ". . . The Conference [*i.e.* the Intergovernmental Conference at which the Single Act was negotiated] requests the Council to give the Advisory Committee procedure in particular a predominant place in the interests of speed and efficiency in the decision-making process, for the exercise of the powers of implementation conferred on the Commission within the field of Article 100A [*i.e.* the Internal Market] of the EEC Treaty."

Unfortunately, as so often happened, the Council of Ministers was not prepared to implement what their own Heads of Government had decided and they have over the years continued to insist on Regulatory Committees. Nevertheless, good government demands that the powers of the Commission in this area should be reinforced and strengthened: and the Council of Ministers confined to its proper legislative role.

## Membership of the Commission

When the Community was founded the Commission had nine members, two for each of the three large Member

States, France, Germany and Italy, and one each for the three small states, Belgium, Netherlands and Luxembourg, which had originally formed the Benelux Union. In terms of population this pattern favoured the Benelux countries whose total population was little more than half that of any one of the three large states. This was deliberate and runs right through all the institutions. Power and voting was loaded in favour of the three small countries to give them the assurance that they would not be oppressed by the large Member States. This "weighting" of the Benelux vote has always been a source of difficulty when new Member States have joined and it still remains a source of grievance on the part of those who do not know the history and the reasons.

When I joined the Commission it had 14 members: the accession of Spain and Portugal increased this to 17, Spain counting as a large Member State with two Commissioners and Portugal securing one only. For many years now there has been strong pressure, particularly from the United Kingdom, that the number of Commissioners should be reduced to one for each Member State. This view was accepted by the Intergovernmental Conference responsible for negotiating the Maastricht Treaty but the Treaty itself left the matter over for further consideration although it did provide for the number of Vice Presidents to be reduced from six to one or two. My own view is that it is not self evident that the present tally of 17 Commissioners is an excessive number. The British Cabinet for example normally numbers 21 or 22. The real problem is a different one. Some members of the Commission, probably four or five in all, are grossly overburdened: others do not have a proper day's work. Thus, after I left, my own portfolio was distributed among some five Commissioners and adding the pieces together gave a total annual workload of about 2½ man years. Nor is the public perception helped very much by the fact that in common with all politicians, Commissioners without enough to do tend to go swanning off around the world on what at times are little more than public relations exercises directed more to projecting a personal image than solid achievement of Community value. There are few politicians who can afford to throw stones: but even fewer who are deterred from so doing.

Enlargement of the Community will create real problems. The present framework would just about accommodate the four EFTA countries who have successfully applied for Community membership (Austria, Finland, Sweden and Norway): but that would be about the limit. The present intention is that the matter should be dealt with at the Intergovernmental Conference which Article N.2 of the Maastricht Treaty provides should be convened in 1996.

There is no doubt that formal meetings of the Commission are unduly protracted, often extending from nine o'clock in the morning to late at night or even the following morning. There is a tendency for every Commissioner to want to have his say on every subject on the agenda and many of them speak at excessive length. Continental politicians are much addicted to this. Jacques Delors was no exception but his orations were well worthwhile listening to. The same could not be said of many others. I found a Commission of 14, the number when I joined, was very effective. Seventeen, the number after the accession of Spain and Portugal, was just about manageable. A further increase in numbers will create difficulties although in the short term – that is for a year or two – the present arrangements could accommodate the likely maximum four EFTA Commissioners. The answer could well lie very

much on the way that we organise ministerial responsibilities in the United Kingdom, where the senior Minister who is in the Cabinet, is supported by a group of junior
Ministers who are not. Such a solution in the Community
might however raise problems of national susceptibilities
with junior Commissioners being unwilling to accept the
leadership of a senior Commissioner of another
nationality and in some instances actually working against
him. Nevertheless, this was the solution I would have favoured to deal with the impossible weight of my own portfolio had I stayed. Jacques Delors had made it clear that if
I was not reappointed, neither the United Kingdom nor
anyone else would inherit my position. When I was not
reappointed, he did precisely what he had said and my
portfolio was dispersed among a number of Commissioners. Unfortunately, this meant that there was no opportunity of trying out what would have been my favoured
solution and which could well have pointed the way to a
solution of the Commission problem generally.

There are some politicians, particularly in the United
Kingdom and in the European Parliament, who decry
Commissioners as "civil servants", a description no doubt
intended to be a derogatory term of abuse. Commissioners are not civil servants: they are one of the Community institutions with their position entrenched under
the Treaties and ranking equally with the other institutions of the Community. On a personal plane many are
themselves distinguished former politicians in their own
countries, more distinguished than their critics and some
indeed go back into political life in their own countries
when they leave the Commission.

The Treaty, in Article 157, provides clearly and specifically for the independence of the Commissioners. That
alone should dispose of any argument that they are civil

servants. They shall, the article says, "be chosen on the grounds of their general competence and whose independence is beyond doubt". They must act, the article goes on to say, "in the general interest of the Communities, be completely independent in the performance of their duties" and "they shall neither seek nor take instructions from any government or from any other body". The article does in fact go much further than this. Most people stop at the point I have mentioned, not least because it is the end of the page in some of the consolidated texts of the Treaties and apparently therefore the end of the article. If one turns the page over one finds the following:

> "Each Member State undertakes to respect this principle and not to seek to influence the members of the Commission in the performance of their tasks."

This particular quirk of printing layout has led many people to assume that the obligation was one way only, *i.e.* the Commissioner had to be independent: and they overlook what I regard as even more important, namely the obligation on Member States "not to seek to influence" the members of the Commission.

As in all walks of life the degree of independence shown by individual Commissioners varies greatly. But to be fair one must start by accepting that we all bring with ourselves a baggage of preconceived ideas, outlooks and prejudices, many of them of a specific national nature. An Englishman does not think in the same way as a Frenchman, nor does a German share the same prejudices as an Italian. What may at first sight appear to be a nationalistic motive may in fact be the honest expression of individual prejudices.

Nevertheless one must accept that, contrary to their duty, governments do exert pressure on their Commissioners. Although here again, as with all lobbying activities, the dividing line between "information" and "influence" can be a very narrow one. Thus when I first joined the Commission the UK Permanent Representative thought it was his function to see me before every Commission meeting to acquaint me with his government's "views" on the various items on the agenda. He no doubt thought he was simply keeping me properly informed. But to me he was trying to tell me what to do and I quickly disabused him of any idea that he was entitled so to do. I have no doubt that he – or his office – continued to "brief" my *Cabinet*: and if I in my turn wanted to know what the UK Government thought I would ask and preferably by calling on the Minister responsible in London. But I have no doubt that I was a great deal more independent than most Commissioners and while this did not endear me to some elements in London, it was an invaluable asset in dealing with other Member States.

Under the terms of the Treaty Commissioners are chosen by "common accord": but in practice the choice of a Commissioner rests in the hands of the Member State concerned. Here again the general air of hostility to the Community by successive governments in the United Kingdom has been unhelpful and counter-productive. On the Continent, senior politicians will move from their national Parliaments to the Community institutions and back again and this can be regarded as the natural development of a political career. Thus, Jacques Delors himself has been a senior Minister in the French Government, a member of the European Parliament and then President of the Commission: and his ambitions are said to extend to becoming President of France. Martin Bangemann has been a Member of the European Parliament, a senior Minister in the Federal Republic and now

Vice President of the Commission: and anyone who thought that would be the end of his career is likely to be mistaken. Giscard d'Estaing, former President of France, has resurfaced as a Member of the European Parliament, as has Willy de Clercq, former Belgian Minister and Member of the Commission. In contrast to this no British Commissioner has ever effectively been able to re-enter British political life with any great success: most indeed have never been able to surmount the first hurdle of securing a seat in Parliament again. A ticket to Brussels tends to be a one way ticket and no up and coming politician with attractive prospects before him at Westminster is likely happily to accept being drafted to Brussels. I personally had the immense advantage that my political ambitions were spent: and I always had my seat in the House of Lords to return to.

## The Commission as the driving force of the Community

The Commission is the driving force of the Community. Where a country such as France or Italy with a very strong European commitment holds the Presidency, the Presidency can and does make a very significant contribution. But almost invariably the lead is given by the Commission as it has been in the case of the Internal Market, Monetary Union, Social Policy and Political Union to name but a few. If the Commission is ineffective, as tragically it was during the Thorne Presidency (1980–84), the Community languishes. Where you have a forceful and visionary President, as Jacques Delors has been, backed by a strong and effective Commission, the Community makes progress. The Commission has an enormous armoury of powers at its disposal: not only for example the right of initiative but the fact that it can only be overruled by the Council by unanimity. Measures, particularly in the Internal Market field, may only require a majority for adoption. But to change the Commission's proposals requires unanimity and this provides an invaluable bargaining position for the Commission in the negotiations over any proposal before the Council. The Commission can always amend its proposals if it so wishes, but can only be forced to do so by unanimity: and an offer by the Commission to amend on a point of special interest to a particular Member State may be the payment the Member State will willingly accept in return for supporting the proposal as a whole. The Commission's rights in this respect extend to specifying the legal base, *i.e.* the provision in the Treaty under which a proposal is put forward. The Commission will always choose an article requiring majority voting if it conceivably can, thus side stepping a small recalcitrant minority and its right to do so has been upheld by the Court of Justice. Some Member States, and unfortunately the United Kingdom is one of the worst offenders, constantly try to add an article, for example Article 235, which requires unanimity to the legal base and they do so in order to try and block the measure. The Court of Justice, however, has decided that a sole legal base is permissible if it covers the main purpose of a proposal and that it is not necessary to add Article 235, which is a kind of "catch all" provision, to cover subsidiary matters.

The Commission's powers and position are greatly reinforced by the fact that it is legally entitled to attend all meetings of the European Parliament and to speak (Art 140) and under Article 155 it is entitled to "participate in the shaping of measures" taken by the Council and the Parliament. Now under the terms of Article 2 of the Single European Act, reinforced by the provisions of the

Maastricht Treaty, the President of the Commission is a full member of the European Council in parallel with the Heads of State or Government of the Member States and a member of the Commission is entitled to attend on the same basis as the Foreign Ministers.

When the Single European Act was being negotiated I warned Jacques Delors that any extension of the powers of the Parliament must not be at the expense of the Commission: that what had happened over the years was that the Council had gradually encroached upon the powers of the Commission: and that what was needed was an increase in the Parliament's powers at the expense of the Council: in contrast, to allow it to increase its powers at the expense of the Commission would simply exacerbate the imbalance which had already been created between the institutions and that must not be allowed to happen. In the event the increase in the Parliament's powers which was conceded was not very great and was largely at the expense of the Council – namely through the introduction of the "co-operation procedure". The Parliament was bitterly disappointed at what it felt to be an inadequate increase in its powers and it blamed the Commission. It was a short sighted and perverse reaction as the Commission has always been the Parliament's staunchest ally.

The problem has not gone away and indeed it became a very live issue in the negotiation over Political Union. The Parliament has now achieved a degree of suzerainty over the Commission. Article 144 of the Treaty of Rome had given the Parliament the power by a two-thirds majority provided that in turn was an absolute majority of the total membership, to censure the Commission as a body and the Commission was then required to resign. Some members of the Parliament claimed that this meant that the Commission is under the "political control" of the

Parliament. The argument is nonsense. I did in fact question Emile Noel, who was Secretary General of the Commission for 30 years, indeed ever since the Treaty of Rome was signed, about the reasons for Article 144. The story he told me was that the drafters of the Treaty felt that if some intolerable situation arose there must be some means of ousting the Commission and replacing it by another: it was impossible to vest this power in the Council as that would subject the Commission to pressures from the Member States and deprive it of its independence which the Treaty had been at such pains to protect. *Faux de mieux* therefore the power was vested in the Parliament in the confidence that it would never be needed or used. The parallel which tends now to be drawn with the power of a national Parliament to bring down its own national government did not enter into the matter at all: nor would it have been a compelling precedent as in those days the European Parliament was not elected but appointed. Like all Doomsday powers the power vested in the European Parliament has never been used. When I first came to the Commission I was horrified to find that some of my fellow Commissioners treated threats by the Parliament – or more accurately by individual members – seriously. When they quoted Article 144 to me, I reminded them of what had happened to Samson.

The Parliament's stance is based essentially on its claim to be the only one of the Community institutions with democratic legitimacy. The Maastricht Treaty now goes some way to meeting the Parliament's demands. Under Article 158 of that Treaty, the Member States must consult the European Parliament before appointing the President of the Commission: and the President and the other members of the Commission "shall be subject as a body to a vote of approval by the European Parliament" before they are formally appointed. The term of office of the Commission is now lined up with that of Parliament, *i.e.* five years and a Commission now takes office in the January following the election of a Parliament in the preceding June. It should be noted that the "approval" by the Parliament extends to the Commission as a body: the Parliament cannot approve some Commissioners and reject others, although experience shows it may attempt to do so.

It is a matter of some regret that in the last year or two the Commission has found itself in conflict with a number of Member States, particularly the United Kingdom, over what is claimed to be an excessive use of its powers. There is something in this criticism although it must be said that the attitude of the United Kingdom is primarily a reflection of internal difficulties inside the Conservative Party and an attempt to find a scapegoat to divert attention and deflect criticism from its own supporters. Nevertheless, one must accept that in the last year or two the Commission has at times adopted too aggressive a role both in relation to the subject matter of the Intergovernmental Conferences and on day to day matters. Unfortunately the Commission is not as cohesive as it was in my day: it does not act so much as a College: individual members have tended to run off on their own, sometimes almost out of control: and (and I greatly regret having to say so) Jacques Delors himself, with his numerous other preoccupations has not been able to exercise the degree of control that he did in the first Delors Commission of which I was a member. But there has also been a sea change in public attitudes. People generally are more distrustful of governments, whether the "government" is their own national government or the Community. They resent interference in their private lives and if that "interference" comes from a body over which they have little or no control, they resent the interference even more. At least they can get rid of national governments and frequently do. But the Community is more remote and less vulnerable. This is a matter which needs to be tackled and the introduction of the principle of "subsidiarity" into the Maastricht Treaty is an attempt to do so.

## The European Parliament

The legislative function is shared between the European Parliament and the Council of Ministers. The Parliament represents the people, as does the House of Representatives in the United States. The Council of Ministers represents the states, in just the same way as the Senate does in America. Originally the Parliament was appointed from the ranks of parliamentarians in the Member States but since 1979 it has been directly elected. It is supposed to be elected on a uniform voting system but no uniform system has yet been agreed; nevertheless, the fact is that 11 of the 12 Member States adopt some form of proportionate representation, only the United Kingdom adopting the "first past the post" system.

The European Parliament started life with the unfortunate label of "Assembly" hung around its neck. I have always taken the view that this was a mistranslation – or at best an unfortunate translation. The Treaties of course were written in French and in France the Parliament is the *Assemblée Nationale.* As a matter of interest, the French dictionary, *Robert,* defines the British House of Commons as an *assemblée* and it is the House of Lords and House of Commons taken together which constitute the *Parlement.* Unfortunately in colloquial English "assembly" carries a somewhat derogatory connotation: an inferior body, or as for example in the term "riotous assembly" even an undesirable one. The (then) Prime Minister herself fell into this trap and in a conversation with Geoffrey Howe and myself dismissed the European Parliament as "a mere Assembly" only to be somewhat tentatively corrected by Geoffrey Howe pointing out that the name had been changed by the Single European Act to the "European Parliament". This indeed is the case, although the Single Act does it in a somewhat circuitous way; Article 3, which is concerned with the powers of the institutions, includes a subordinate phrase which refers to the institutions "henceforth designated as referred to hereafter" and then in Article 4 simply uses the term "the European Parliament": in short, correcting an error rather than changing a name.

The European Parliament's main function, in its own eyes, is increasing its own powers. There is in principle nothing unusual about this: the Parliament at Westminster has been doing it at least since 1642 and having now run out of opportunities of seizing the powers of the executive has turned its attention to seizing the powers of the local authorities. To its horror it is now seeing its own powers being pre-empted by the Community, which, as much in fear as in anger, and with scant respect for accuracy it contemptuously refers to as "Brussels". Originally the European Parliament had two significant functions only. Together with the Council, it constituted the budgetary authority: but in other matters it could only deliver an "opinion". But as has happened with all Parliaments, not least the Westminster Parliament, it has used, or even abused, its powers in a way designed to increase its influence. By blocking the budget and threatening a crisis in the Community, it has often extracted concessions from the Council of Ministers. But its greatest progress has been made by the device of withholding its opinion until its demands are met. The tactic is based on the judgment of the Court of Justice in the *Isogluconate* case. In that case the Council plunged ahead without waiting for the Parliament's opinion. The Court held that the Council was in the wrong. The judgment is nothing like as strong or as clear cut as the Parliament has claimed. The Council had behaved with arrogance and unnecessary haste and the Parliament had not been given any real opportunity of expressing its opinion. The legal advice given after this judgment both to the Council of Ministers and to the Commission was that if the Parliament was given ample opportunity, and despite reminders still did not express an opinion, the Court would as likely as not take the view that the Parliament had no opinion to express. I suspect that the cooler heads in the Parliament took much the same view. In the only case where we reached the crunch point when I was in the Commission where the Parliament thrice rejected a proposal which the outgoing President of the Commission had promised the German Government he would introduce, the President of the Parliament tactfully retreated when Jacques Delors and I saw him. Nevertheless, the delaying tactics the Parliament could legitimately employ meant that the Commission was often ready to back amendments proposed by the Parliament in order to make progress. But once the Parliament had given its opinion, its powers were spent, as, before the Single Act, the Council was under no obligation to pay regard to the Parliament's amendments and commonly did not do so.

The Single Act marked a significant change by the introduction of the "co-operation procedure". This applied not only to the Internal Market and matters related thereto, but also to certain aspects of Social Policy, the

Structural Funds and Science and Technology. Under the co-operation procedure, the Parliament gave two readings to the proposals – usually in the form of Directives – which came to it. On the first reading it could if it so wished amend the proposals by a simple majority. If the Commission accepted the Parliament's amendments the proposal as amended went to the Council of Ministers. The Council would then adopt a "common position" either accepting or rejecting the Parliament's amendments and, usually, making further amendments of its own. The proposal as now amended would return to the Parliament. The Parliament in turn could accept the Council's amendments or it could reject them, but to reject it required an absolute majority of all of its members, not simply of those voting. Finally the proposal returned to the Council. What happened then was the subject of further detailed rules involving the participation of the Commission. The rules were not watertight and a situation could occur where the proposal lapsed because agreement could not be reached and the rules failed to deal with such a contingency. The whole procedure appeared complex and fraught with endless possibility of delay, obstruction and deadlock. As so often happens in the Community, the lack of precision reflected an inability by the Member States to agree how procedural problems should be solved. I was extremely apprehensive about the outcome. But while it greatly added to my own workload, no serious problem arose during my own term of office. After a great deal of sabre rattling by the Parliament and a display of arrogance by the Council, matters settled down and we established an effective working relationship with the Commission acting as honest broker between the other two institutions. The Maastricht Treaty has now further strengthened the powers of the Parliament by giving it, in effect, a right of veto in certain areas, thus placing the Council in the position that it either accommodates the views of the Parliament or the legislation is lost altogether.

The quality of membership of the Parliament varies enormously. There are some very good MEPs (Members of the European Parliament) of all nationalities, able hardworking and dedicated to the success of the Community. It was both a pleasure and an honour to work with them. Unfortunately there are some very bad ones too. The tragedy is that it is the bad ones who attract the press headlines, which is what they set out to do. The Parliament has insufficient real authority to occupy its time productively and as a result it gives endless attention to matters which have little to do with it and over which it can exercise neither control nor influence. On more than one occasion I have had important Internal Market matters pushed off the agenda in favour of some acrimonious debate on what is happening in some remote country in some obscure part of the world. As foreign policy is not a matter of Community competence, the Parliament has no *locus standi* and they can do nothing about it, however strongly they may feel as individuals. It is this irrelevance which has done the European Parliament so much damage in the public eye, and particularly in the United Kingdom. It is a tragedy because so often it pushes into obscurity the good work, and at times the exceptional good work, the Parliament does do. There is a real dilemma here. Because of its restricted powers and influence, the Parliament does not always attract parliamentarians of an adequate calibre; but so long as Members of the European Parliament rightly or wrongly are seen in the eyes of national politicians to be of inferior calibre, there is a reluctance on the part of Member States to increase the powers of the Parliament in a way which would attract the best candidates.

Our own position, that is the position of the British MEPs, in the European Parliament has never been a happy one. Our Socialist members through most of the time I was in the Commission were opposed to the Community and to British membership. Their subsequent conversion was based not on principle but on antipathy to Mrs Thatcher. No one really believed it and most of them did not themselves. They belonged to the main Socialist grouping in the Parliament but were viewed with suspicion and embarrassment. The position of the Conservatives was little better. The mainstream Centre Right grouping, the Christian Democrats, would have nothing to do with them. Physically they were even pushed out to the far right in the Chamber where seats are allocated to parties in the Hemicycle according to their political complexion. But more recently there has been a thawing of relations. Single handed Mrs Thatcher lost the European Parliamentary Elections in June 1989. The Conservative Party was decimated and the Labour victory gave the Socialists an overall majority in the European Parliament. But there was a silver lining to the cloud. The Centre Right began to look upon the British Conservatives as innocent victims of Mrs Thatcher's misplaced views and there was a great deal of personal sympathy for them. The British Conservatives in turn have moved further to the centre of European politics than the government in Westminster.

After a period of probation they have been accepted into the fold of the Christian Democratic Group although on the basis of a declaration on policy matters much more *communautaire* than the official policy of the Conservative Party. The adoption by the Christian Democratic Group in the European Parliament of a manifesto for the 1994

European Elections with a strong "European" flavour is set fair to produce real difficulties once again.

In looking at the future role of the Parliament, there is one very important factor to bear in mind. There is a fundamental difference between the European Parliament and national Parliaments whether in Europe or America. None of the proposals considered by the Intergovernmental Conference addressed this problem. In national Parliaments there is always a party, or parties, supporting the government and a party or parties opposing it. It is this conflict or tension which gives Parliaments their real cutting edge and relevance. There is none of this in the European Parliament. There is no "government party", not least because the Community has no "government" in the proper sense of the term. As a result the Parliament tends simply to be "agin the government" whether you regard the "government" as the Commission or the Council of Ministers. Alliances will be formed on individual issues, sometimes supportive of the Commission or the Council, sometimes against it. But there is nothing in the nature of a coherent "government" policy covering all important aspects of economic and social life and other major issues, one party or group dedicated to support it and another to oppose it. It is this lack of "focus" from which the Parliament suffers which accounts for much of its apparent irrelevance and prevents it playing a decisive role in Community affairs. The provisions in the Maastricht Treaty to give the Parliament a say in the appointment of the President and the members of the Commission will not change this situation. It will be, in a sense, a "one off" event. The most that could be said will be that the President and the members of the Commission enjoyed the broad confidence of the Commission and that their objectives in broad policy terms were acceptable to the Parliament. But that will be all. Individual issues, however important, will still be dealt with on an *ad hoc* basis with alliances forming and dissolving. Certainly there will be nothing in the nature of a "Commission Party", *i.e.* a political party committed to supporting the Commission, evolving in the Parliament.

## The Council of Ministers

The Council shares the legislative function with the Parliament but it is by far and away the more important partner. The Commission proposes: the Parliament may amend: but it is the Council which decides. Unfortunately only too often it has failed to decide. The Council represents the Member States: legally it is the most powerful of all the Community institutions: but in general it fails to exercise its powers in the interests of the Community: only too often it simply uses its powers in the interests of individual Member States.

The Treaty speaks of "the Council" as though a single body was contemplated. In fact innumerable "specialist" Councils have been spawned – nearly 30 at the latest count – representing the various fields of activity falling within Community competence – the Council of Finance Ministers, known as ECOFIN, the Agricultural Council, the Industry Council, the Internal Market Council: and so on almost *ad infinitum*: and even some fields of activity where there was at the time no Community competence, for example the Cultural Council, although that particular Council has now, in effect, been legitimised by the Maastricht Treaty.

These Councils are made up of Ministers from the corresponding Departments in the Member States: thus

ECOFIN consists of the 12 Finance Ministers, the Agricultural Council the 12 Ministers of Agriculture and so on. But in some Councils membership ebbs and flows between different Ministers: thus, the Internal Market Council would bring together Trade Ministers, Ministers of the Economy, Interior Ministers and so on depending on the particular business in hand. In addition to these "specialist" Councils there is also a General Affairs Council attended by the Foreign Ministers and for this reason sometimes referred to as the Foreign Affairs Council. The General Affairs Council *inter alia* prepares the agenda for the meetings of the European Council, that is the meetings of the Heads of Government. During my term of office in the Commission we tried to get this Council, as the senior Council, to exercise some sort of control over the specialist Councils, but they declined. Some departmental Ministers, for example Ministers of Agriculture, are very powerful Ministers in their own country and unwilling and unlikely to accept a degree of suzerainty by their Foreign Ministers.

The real trouble with the Council – and I deliberately use the omnibus term – is that it consists of departmental Ministers whose main objective in life is to protect not just their national interests but their departmental interests as well. Thus, the Ministers of Agriculture regard it as their primary function to protect the farmers, which traditionally meant giving them as much money as was needed to maintain an ever expanding and prosperous agricultural sector, leaving it to someone else to pick up the bill. After Fontainebleau (in June 1984), the concept was that the Finance Ministers should exercise some control over total expenditure on agriculture, but to put it bluntly they declined to shoulder this unpopular burden. In the end it has always been the Heads of Government who have had to be brought in to make the Ministers of Agriculture behave in a financially responsible manner. It may be thought that in reaching agreement in 1992–93 on reform of the Common Agricultural Policy, partly in the context of the GATT negotiations, the Agricultural Council had acquitted itself well. Certainly much better than in the past: but it required constant prodding by the Heads of Government to secure agreement and experience will almost certainly show that the reforms agreed are inadequate. Certainly inadequate in terms of cutting down the cost of the CAP to an acceptable level.

I cite the Agricultural Council because it is the clearest example but it would be wrong to acquit other Councils of "conduct unbecoming". I had perhaps less trouble with the Internal Market Council than most partly because its whole ethos was a European one in which the European interest as often as not coincided with the national interest: and also because of the constant impetus to progress given by every single meeting of the European Council.

Nor is the way the Council works impressive. One's mental image is that of a dozen distinguished gentlemen sitting around a table trying to thrash out their problems. In fact it is nothing of the sort. Some Ministers arrive in duplicate or triplicate, a senior Minister being supported by various junior Ministers. Everyone has a cohort of officials as well. They arrive late: they read their prepared speeches: and they go home as soon as decency or delicacy permits. Their main objective is to get the business over as soon as they can so that they can catch the next plane home. Few stay beyond 5 p.m., leaving it to officials to carry on in their absence. Unfortunately an official cannot vote so once any sizeable number of Ministers have departed the proceedings degenerate into a talking shop and progress ceases. There are of course exceptions.

Some Ministers are consciencious, hard working and devoted to making a success of the Community and its policies. And a country which holds the Presidency will always make a particular effort as it regards its national dignity and standing involved in a successful Presidency. This is what happened with the British Presidency in 1986: and I always take particular pride in the fact that at the very end of my term of office I was able to coax the Greek Presidency along to produce a result in the Internal Market as good as that produced by the Germans, something that no one would have believed possible: there was ample goodwill on the Greek side: all I had to do was to provide the technical expertise and the necessary impetus.

The meetings of the Council of Ministers are alleged to be "confidential". With the teeming masses present, confidentiality would in any event be impossible. But far worse some Ministers, and ours have been among the worst offenders, make a habit of slipping out of meetings just before they end to give the press highly coloured accounts of what has been going on, to their own greater glory and the confusion of those they regard as their enemies.

It was in the light of experiences of this kind that I came to the firm conclusion that the public interest demanded that the Council should meet in public, its proceedings recorded as happens in our own Parliament and published. This is probably the most important single reform that could be made. It would not only enable the public at large to know what was going on, it would also reveal the extent to which Ministers were attending to their duties. If in addition and reflecting the practice in our own Parliament in Westminster, there was a rule requiring a Minister always to be in attendance and removing Permanent Representatives and officials from the floor of the Council Chamber, the Council could be well on the way to operating efficiently and effectively. In the light of the difficulties over the Maastricht Treaty, a decision was taken at the Edinburgh Summit in December 1992 that measures should be adopted to make the working of the Community institutions, and particularly the Council of Ministers, more transparent. Predictably, the Council of Ministers has itself obstructed the measures needed to give effect to this decision by their own Heads of Government, to such an extent that the Netherlands is now threatening to take the Council to the European Court of Justice.

It may come as somewhat of a surprise, in the light of what has already been said, if I conclude by saying that on the whole I enjoyed remarkably good relations with all the Councils with which I worked. But it would be no good service to them, or to the Community, if I failed to draw attention to the defects of the system and suggest how it might be improved.

## The democratic deficit and the future of the institutions

One of the arguments developed by the European Parliament in recent years relates to what is known as "the democratic deficit". The proposition has been advanced of course primarily as a ploy to justify the Parliament's claim to greater powers. The argument is that the Parliament is elected while neither the Council nor the Commission is. It is this "democratic deficit" in the Community which it is claimed can only be rectified by according "top dog" status to the Parliament. Hence the demands that the Commission be appointed by the Parliament and should be answerable to the Parliament: that the Parliament should be given an equal right of initiative with the Commission; and that it should have equal status with the Council in matters of legislation. The first of these claims, relating to the appointment of the Commission has been watered down and it now appears in the Maastricht Treaty in the form I have indicated, namely that the Parliament has to approve the appointment of the President before the appointment is made and confirm, *ex post*, the appointment of the President and the members of the Commission.

There is some truth in the talk of a "democratice deficit" as a matter of analysis but the position is not as clear cut as the Parliament tries to argue. The Ministers who form the Council of Ministers are themselves elected in their own countries: the members of the Commission are normally serving politicians at the time they are appointed and most of them have occupied or at the time of their appointment or nomination do occupy senior ministerial posts. I realise that my own position was anomalous in that I am a member of the House of Lords but that is a quirk of the British Constitution and nothing to do with the European Parliament.

But it would in my view be completely wrong to subject the Commission to the control of the Parliament, which would fly in the face of the basic principles of the Treaty. The independence of the Commission from the legislature is an essential element in the institutional balance and it accords with strict constitutional theory. Nevertheless, the argument about the unelected nature of the Commission will not go away and a solution needs to be found.

## "To whom?" is the important issue

I would only make this one final comment to conclude this review of the institutions of the Community. In discussing the future of the Community we tend to concentrate on the policies and powers of the Community – on Economic and Monetary Union, security and defence and so forth. But increasingly, I have come to the conclusion that just as important, or indeed more important than what powers should be transferred to the Community, is the question of to whom those powers should be transferred. This is why I have· dealt with these institutional matters in greater detail than would otherwise have been appropriate in a treatise of this kind. It is only if we understand how these matters work and what are the real problems and deficiencies that we are likely to be able to forge an acceptable and durable solution.

## Chapter 8
# The Thatcher Years and the Single Market

I served my time with the Commission during the Thatcher years and it is all too easy therefore to equate criticism of the attitude of the United Kingdom to the Community with criticism of the Thatcher Government as such. This would be too shallow a conclusion as our difficulties with the Community go much deeper than that.

Our failure to join the Community as a founding member was just as much the fault of the post war Labour Government which was responsible for our refusal to join the original Coal and Steel Community – the first of the "Communities": and of the Macmillan Conservative Government which refused to participate in the Messina Conference or in the European Economic Community which was the product of that Conference. Throughout, the motives were mixed: or perhaps it might be more accurate to say an amalgam of disparate motives. We emerged from the war as a victorious but exhausted power but still retaining the remnants of our glory and some contempt for the Continental countries. We had involved ourselves reluctantly in the wars of the mainland powers, as we had in 1914, and as in 1918 we were only too glad to have our soldiers home and once again our hope, never this time quite realised, was to retreat once more within our island fortress. What we had seen in the first half of the present century mirrored our history of many, many centuries past. For nigh on 1,000 years this country had not seriously been invaded. We had fought our wars on other people's territory, it had been their cities destroyed, their populations starved and decimated. Our motives had never reflected any element of idealism: our guiding principle had been the maintenance of the "balance of power" which meant ensuring that no single Continental country ever dominated Europe as a whole. So we switched sides whenever expediency dictated. Once the war was over we retreated to our island fortress, pulled up the drawbridge – at least until the next time when we felt ourselves threatened by the emergence of a new, dominant power in Europe. The 1939–45 war was the most traumatic of all but also, in important respects, very different. Our cities were bombed, tens of thousands of our citizens at home killed and hundreds of thousands injured. We had been in imminent risk of invasion with all the horrors of war brought home to us on our own doorstep. Although in a sense this was a shared experience with our Continental allies, our reaction after the war was very different from theirs. We were prepared to station our troops on the Continent to ensure that peace was preserved first against our enemies and later against our old ally Russia. But we never shared the vision of the founders of the Community that peace could only be preserved by co-operation and ultimately "union" between former enemies. From the outset we remained outsiders. The English Channel was never just a physical barrier: it was a psychological barrier as well.

We joined the Community in a brief outburst of enthusiasm in 1973 under the leadership of Ted Heath. But he lasted only a few months after our accession. In

February 1974 he was succeeded as Prime Minister by Mr Harold Wilson. The Labour Party was, and until very recently remained, opposed in principle to the European Community. Wilson was a supreme pragmatist, or opportunist. Once in power he realised the difficulties of withdrawal from the Community and he directed his fire therefore to a "renegotiation" of our terms of entry. This tactic enabled him to score points off the Conservative Party who were pilloried for having been too soft in the accession negotiations while at the same time avoiding the disaster of withdrawal. But of course *vis à vis* our fellow members it meant that five years were wasted in confrontation and quarrel which contributed mightily to the paralysis of the Community and bitterly affronted all those who had hoped that British membership would give the Community a new impetus and offset the domination of the Franco-German axis. The victory of Mrs Thatcher and the Conservative Party in 1979 did not improve matters. Determined as she was to slash public expenditure, our contribution to the Community budget was a particular target. Of course there was real substance in her view that our contribution was excessive. But that was clearly foreseeable when we agreed to join the Community in 1972. Mrs Thatcher was then a member of the Cabinet and was therefore a party to the decision to join and on the basis of the terms then negotiated. Moreover, what had gone wrong could well be said to be the fault of the British economy and of the British Government. The calculation had been that the opening up of the European market to British industry could more than outweigh the cost in terms of our contribution. This is precisely what had happened in the case of Germany. The "marriage contract" of the Community, as it was described by Jacques Delors, was that Germany should shoulder the cost of supporting

French agriculture in return for German industry being given free access to the French market. The bargain proved to be greatly to Germany's advantage. Although it became, and remains, the largest net contributor to the Community's funds, it also became the most powerful industrial power in the Community. We had hoped to see a similar outcome. We were to be bitterly disappointed. Whether one places the blame on the shoulders of government or accepts that British attitudes in industry, on both sides, were largely to blame is, in the present context, immaterial. The fact is that we were lumbered with the contributions but never garnered the *quid pro quo* in industrial success.

Mrs Thatcher secured a temporary rebate at Dublin in December 1979. The failure at Athens in March 1983 led to an outburst of anti-Community anger with threats of withdrawal quenched only – and interestingly – by the Prime Minister herself saying that as a Party we had invested so much political capital in the Community and with an election only a few months away it was impossible to change tack now. Fortunately the failure at Athens largely reflected the inability of the Greeks, lacking any previous experience, to manage a meeting of the Heads of Government: and the following year at Fontainebleau a quasi-permanent settlement – which still endures – was reached. I personally regarded the settlement as fair, even generous. It was certainly a great triumph over deeply entrenched opposition. It opened a window of opportunity with the Prime Minister vindicated and triumphant and it was in that warm glow of victory I agreed to go to Brussels.

But it did not last. I have already described the actual course of events. What I am concerned with here is analysing the attitudes and underlying causes which led to those events.

Deep down Mrs Thatcher was throughout opposed to the Community. Ted Heath's reaction to his defeat as leader of the Conservative Party at her hands was matched only by her antipathy to him. He had taken us into the Community: therefore the Community was bad. The fact that she had been party to our accession was rejected as irrelevant, even if remembered. She never understood the Community, neither its philosophy, its motivation, nor indeed its actual policies and legal provisions. Like Ted Heath, my life had spanned both of the Great Wars of the present century. At heart perhaps we had much in common with the founders of the Community in believing that the preservation of the peace meant that former enemies had to come together on the basis of a new and enduring compact. Understandably, Mrs Thatcher had no such background and she never shared the reaction of those directly involved in these events that we must build a new Europe. To her it was just history and a history of the defeat of our enemies. Some members of her entourage still regarded them as the country's enemies and as her initial reaction to German unification showed, she sympathised with their views.

Her protracted battle and ultimate success over the British budget contribution merely served to confirm her views of the other members of the Community. There was no generosity in her reaction, no recognition that the hatchet was now buried and we were friends and allies. Merely a haunting suspicion waiting for the next round of European perfidy at Britain's expense.

Her support for the Internal Market Programme, the Single Market as it became to be called in the United Kingdom, was largely based on a misunderstanding. She was convinced throughout that the Community was simply a free trade area with one or two additions such as the

Common Agricultural Policy to which she strongly objected. Indeed one of her senior Ministers described it publicly in these terms. Interestingly, in a recent speech (at Brussels on 10 December 1993) Federal Chancellor Kohl is reported as having said:

> "I have never understood Mrs Thatcher who believes that the future of Europe lies in a super free trade area."

It was only as the Single Market Programme gradually unfolded she realised that it intruded into areas she was determined to keep entirely in her own hands. She seemed unaware of the fact that many of these matters were specifically provided for in the Treaties or had become part of the Community "*acquis*" before we joined and that we were bound under the Treaty of Accession to abide by them. It was not simply that she was not cognizant of these matters, she simply did not believe them and very often claimed that the position was precisely the opposite of what the law and the Treaties clearly said. She was a lawyer and indeed had made her reputation attacking in great detail, and to devastating effect, the tax proposals of the Labour Government in 1974 and 1975. She had essentially the tax lawyer's outlook: not how to give effect to the intention of the Statute, but how to avoid it. She misunderstood the whole concept of "unanimity". Its true purpose was to enable all the Member States to make progress together. She regarded it simply as a right of veto. She was not alone on this point but her attitude was the most uncompromising. And it was this which led ultimately to Britain being marginalised and driven into defeat as happened over the Single European Act and later over the Delors package of reforms which was finally agreed at the second Brussels Summit in February 1988. We see the same point resurrected in the recent dispute over voting rights in the case of the present (1994) enlargement negotiations.

The more it became apparent that the Internal Market Programme inevitably meant that the Community collectively, rather than Member States individually, had to take the lead in legislating, the stronger Mrs Thatcher's opposition became. Her opposition to Labour Party policies, which she regarded as having ruined the country, was reflected in a passionate attachment to deregulation, to voluntary self regulation and a deeply ingrained hostility to bureaucracy. She never seemed to realise that the Internal Market Programme meant that all 12 Member States had to conform to a common set of rules and this meant in turn that the rules had to be embodied in legislation and that legislation had to be enforced by a judicial process. She was quick enough to criticise other Member States for failing to abide by the rules but she would never accept that the only way of meeting her own complaint was by legislation by the Community. Nor would she ever accept that the Brussels "bureaucracy" was very small by comparison with her own bureaucracy in the United Kingdom, that in any event one bureaucracy to deal with a Community-wide issue was smaller than 12 separate national bureaucracies and that much of the passionate pursuit of detail by her own Ministers was itself a potent cause of bureaucracy.

As it became evident that the Internal Market Programme was bound to lead ultimately to Economic and Monetary Union and even in the eyes of some to Social Policy – just as the Solemn Declaration and the Single European Act provided – the greater her opposition became. The fact that she had signed the former and pushed the latter through the Parliament at Westminster did not help. She felt that she had been conned into so doing and she vented her anger on those she felt responsible.

Her attitude to the Solemn Declaration which she herself had signed is puzzling. After I had returned to the United Kingdom I was questioned on this (in 1989) by the Select Committee of the House of Commons on European Legislation. I was reminded by the Chairman, Mr Nigel Spearing, that at the time (1983) I was a member of Cabinet and he asked me what had been the reaction of the Cabinet to the Solemn Declaration. It is worth quoting the Minutes of Evidence of the Select Committee on the exchanges which took place.

"Chairman
13. . . . you mentioned the Solemn Declaration on European Union of June 1983?
(Lord Cockfield) That is right.
14. Am I right that you were on that occasion a member of Her Majesty's Government?
(Lord Cockfield) I was.
15. Was that the understanding of the Cabinet at that time. Did you make that clear?
(Lord Cockfield) I think that if you want to know what goes on in Cabinet you have to ask Mr Bernard Ingham. As far as I am concerned, I take the old fashioned view that the proceedings in Cabinet are confidential.
16. I entirely understand your reference. . . ."

My reply was not entirely disingenuous. I could not remember then, and I cannot remember now, whether the matter ever had been reported to Cabinet.

The Falklands War was a major factor both in her dominance in her own government in the United Kingdom and in her attitude to the European Community. She won a very great victory in impossible circumstances and against all the odds. It confirmed her in her antipathy to foreigners of every description, not least to those in Europe: and it recreated in her own mind the picture of Britain triumphant. Nowhere does her attitude come out more clearly than in her General Election Manifesto when she bracketed the European Community with General Galtieri and Mr Arthur Scargill as the dragons she had slain. Our economic weakness, our decline in fortune and influence in the world were all forgotten. To me it seemed increasingly that she saw herself in the image of Lawrence Olivier playing the part of Henry V at the Battle of Agincourt. The champion of Britain and Britain's rights against the world and not least the European Community.

Her failure to stop the progress of the Community became more and more a source of exasperation. Her signature of the Solemn Declaration could be overlooked, or forgotten. Even the Single Act could, however dubiously, be argued away and the reference in the Act to Article 236 of the Treaty, designed in truth to deal with the way progress should be made, could be represented as a right of veto. But this would not last. Her capitulation in February 1988, admittedly at 2 a.m. on the third day of the third Summit on the Delors "package", rankled deeply. Jacques Delors' appearance at the Trade Union Congress in support of the Unions, whose excesses Mrs Thatcher had striven to suppress, genuinely and perhaps justifiably infuriated her.

She endeavoured to buttress her position intellectually by reviving the 19th century concept of national sovereignty and in its more extreme form of sovereignty not by the people as Abraham Lincoln had expressed it but by the Westminster Parliament. She swept away the history of the last 100 years; the declining power both *de facto* and *de jure* of the British Parliament; the growth of international and supranational bodies, not least the European

Community itself, to which sovereignty had been surrendered: and above all the increasing interdependence of the world which cabined and confined any national sovereignty. The full flowering of this approach was seen in her speech at Bruges attacking the Community and its whole philosophy. It made some appeal to the more extreme or archaic elements in the United Kingdom but on the Continent it only served to isolate her even further.

It was not entirely her own fault. Her contacts with the real world were sparse and unreliable. She rarely read the newspapers and relied on what her Press Office chose to tell her. She was surrounded by those sharing her own prejudices and whose views of the world outside were as through a mirror darkly. As she became more and more dictatorial, officials and others increasingly became afraid of telling her the plain, unvarnished truth. I saw some of the dispatches sent to her: they were a travesty of what had really happened and it is not surprising that she confused defeat with victory or failed completely to understand what others were thinking or doing. The scandal over fraud in the Community and the obstructive role the United Kingdom had played, a matter on which I spoke on more than one occasion in the House of Lords, is a clear example of this. Just after I returned from Brussels she erupted in a fit of great anger over fraud in the Community. She was entirely right to do so. But the truth of the matter was that it was her own government, during her own Presidency, which had played a leading role in blocking the attempts made by the Commission, and myself in particular, to deal with this issue. In a memorandum signed by a Senior Minister and circulated to the Council of Ministers the government's opposition was firmly stated. In the words of the memorandum itself "they saw no need" for the measures proposed by the Commission.

Nor did they propose any other measures. When, as a result of the report of the Court of Auditors, the question of fraud came to her attention and she exploded, no one dared tell her of the leading part her own government had played in stopping action being taken. I never received a proper answer to the points I had raised. But then there was no answer which could have been given.

Nor were matters helped by the fact that the information given to Parliament on European affairs was at best incomplete and at times exiguous to the point of being thought misleading. I have already referred to the Solemn Declaration on European Union signed at Stuttgart in June 1983. Despite the fact that it was one of the most important documents in the history of the Community and was to provide much of the impetus for the future development of the Community, it appeared only as "the third matter we discussed" in the Prime Minister's Statement in the House of Commons on the outcome of the Stuttgart Summit (Hansard, 23 June 1983, cols 141/146): it occupied only six and a half lines in a statement extending to a column and a half and, while to be fair, it "welcomed the reaffirmation of the wider objectives of the European Community", it gave no indication of what those "wider objectives" were nor did it foreshadow the fact that in years to come she was bitterly to oppose them. Mr Michael Foot, then leader of the Opposition, contented himself with the banal and misjudged comment that "the best way to describe the outcome of the Stuttgart Council in general is that ... it is extremely disappointing".

The half yearly Report to Parliament on "Developments in the European Community" which might have been expected to flesh out the bald account already given to Parliament, did no better. The Solemn Declaration appeared under the somewhat peculiar heading of "The institutions of the Community": it occupied a bare eight and a half lines: it is described as the "Genscher/Colombo Declaration" as though it was a private initiative by these two distinguished gentlemen: and it was dismissed as "not a legal instrument and involves no Treaty amendments or increases in the powers of the institutions".

All in all it was a monumental misjudgement and it is not surprising that subsequently Mrs Thatcher forgot all about it: and the Select Committee to which I gave evidence appeared never to have heard of it.

The Internal Market Programme fared only marginally better. In the Statement on the Milan Summit to the House of Commons (Hansard, 2 July 1985, cols 185/6) it was bracketed with "strengthening political co-operation and improvements in decision making". The account given amounted to less than one paragraph, some nine lines in all, in a statement extending to one and a half columns of Hansard. There was no reference to the White Paper or to the detailed programme it contained: no reference to the statement in the "Conclusions" of the Summit that the job should be done "completely and effectively": no reference to the freedom of movement of individuals or to the approximation of indirect taxation: despite the fact that all of these matters featured prominently in the "Conclusions" of the Summit. In fairness one must say that the Labour Party was no better informed. Mr Kinnock concentrated on the proposal for the Intergovernmental Conference (which drafted the Single European Act) and the best he could do was to proclaim:

"She got us into this: she is going to have to get us out of it."

But he was wise enough not to try and explain what it was she "got us into" or to say just how "she was going to get us out of it", still less whether it was desirable to do so.

When we come to the corresponding half yearly Report to Parliament on Developments in the European Community, it is just as bad. In a document of 41 pages (or 56 pages if one includes the Appendices) there are just three disjointed references to the Internal Market Programme occupying some 20 lines in all. But the existence of the White Paper detailing the programme did see the light of day in the somewhat cautious comment "The . . . White Paper . . . is being studied". As a reaction to what was to become the standard bearer of the New Europe, the reaction this displayed could hardly be described as enthusiastic.

One can quote many other similar examples but one further and more recent one will suffice. In reporting to the House of Commons on the outcome of the Rome Summit on 27–28 October 1990 the Prime Minister stated that the Council "had to deal in the first place with some urgent items of current business". The statement then proceeded to deal at considerable length with the Common Agricultural Policy, the Uruguay Round, the Gulf and Hungary. When finally it came to deal with Economic and Political Union – under the anodyne heading of "looking further to the future" – the statement was little more than a rehash of the UK's position with no reference at all to the fact that the Summit, on the usual 11 to 1 basis, had come to a firm conclusion on the next steps towards Monetary Union with a specific timetable on Stage 2 of "the Delors Plan" and a commitment to meet in 1997 to prepare the final stage. When one considers that it was these decisions that set in train the events leading to Mrs Thatcher's downfall, one can only wonder

whether to express surprise, dismay or sadness at the un-
balanced nature of the report given to Parliament.

One is at a loss to explain all this. To some extent the
paucity of the information given to Parliament and the
fact that it was so out of focus reflects the Prime Minister's
own outlook and priorities and an obsession with what
were essentially domestic preoccupations. To some extent
it is a reflection of the common psychological problem of
an unwillingness to face up to things one dislikes: a convic-
tion, unsupported by experience, that if you ignore something it will go away. But its effect on public and
parliamentary opinion alike had been damaging to the
national interest and counter productive. It was accompanied throughout the Thatcher era with attempts to
manage the press, particularly through the lobby system.
Why in a free country the press ever allowed themselves to
be manipulated in this way, or the House of Commons
tolerated this viper's nest in its bosom, is a mystery that
only future historians will have sufficient charity to explain. But its legacy is to be seen to this day in a small but
vociferous and even influential anti-European lobby
whose ideas, whose approach and whose rhetoric is based
on an extensive and fundamental lack of understanding
of the facts.

After I left the Commission on 5 January 1989 matters
went from bad to worse. Mrs Thatcher's attitude was forc-
ing the United Kingdom into a position of increasing isolation and ineffectiveness. Her protests were simply
ignored.

The final denouement came over Monetary Union.
After the Madrid Summit in June 1989 which broadly endorsed the Delors Report, she demoted Geoffrey Howe,
blaming him as Foreign Secretary for conning her into
accepting the Madrid Conclusions, as well as for her innu-

merable defeats before. The crunch came with the Rome Summit held in October 1990. I sat in the Peers' Gallery when she reported to the House of Commons. As she read out the prepared statement, drafted by the Foreign Office, I felt with a sense of relief that we were seeing another of her U-turns, the acceptance of the inevitable wrapped up in a great deal of verbiage. But once she started answering questions off the cuff, her old instincts reasserted themselves. Her cry of "No, No, No" echoing across the Chamber was the clearest indication that her judgement had deserted her. Within days, Geoffrey Howe unsheathed the knife which Michael Heseltine plunged between her shoulder blades. In the end the Crown was to be worn by another. But for myself I doubt whether we yet know who will inherit the role of Octavius Caesar.

So she lost the battle and she lost it on her own chosen battleground, Europe. It was a great tragedy. She had been a great Prime Minister. But staying longer than her time she had developed the pride which goes before a fall. And as the Bible says "Great was the fall thereof". The wisdom of the ages has not changed. I hope her successors will learn from her failure. But there is no sign yet that they have. We will be better able to judge that when we come to look at the Maastricht Treaty and what lies beyond.

# Chapter 9
# Beyond the Single Market

The story of the Single Market is a story of success achieved. One often wishes one could stop at a high point of success and devote one's efforts to ensuring the success of what has been achieved. But life is not like that. Success breeds a determination to press ahead and scale the next peak and the one after that; and so on. Indeed I recognised from the beginning, when I said that the Single Market was not the end of the road but the road that led somewhere, that this indeed is what would happen. My work ended when I left the Commission on 5 January 1989 at a time when the Heads of Government had already declared that progress to the completion of the Single Market was now "irreversible". I had done the job I had come to Brussels to do. The baton would now pass into other hands. At the meeting of the Heads of Government at Hannover in June 1988 when Jacques Delors was reappointed President of the Commission, he stressed the advantages of continuity in achieving the successful completion of the Single Market Programme which would flow from my own reappointment. He said:

> " 'On ne change pas une équipe qui gagne'. Cette métaphore sportive aurait pu inspirer la Communauté Européene dans une période marquée par des progrès substantiels dans la réalisation des objectifs de l'Acte Unique, et en particulier

du marché unique de 1992. A ce sujet, précisement, on aurait
espéré pouvior bénéficier de la continuité, garantie que le
movement continuerait au bon rythme, sous la direction de
Lord Cockfield qui a conçu le Livre Blanc sur le grand
marché et l'a mis en oeuvre avec pugnacité et efficacité.''

He went on to make it clear that if I was not reappointed he
would not allow my portfolio to go to another Commissioner and in the event it was split among five Commissioners with Jacques Delors himself taking part. While my
work had come to an end, Jacques Delors himself stayed.
He had much wider ambitions than I had: his ambition was
to see the completion of ''European Union'', in all its aspects of Economic, Monetary and Political Union, during
his time as President of the Commission. It was a grand
ambition and it came within an inch of success. In the end
he was frustrated by events. The Rome Summit in October
1990, which saw agreement on setting up the Intergovernmental Conferences on Economic and Monetary Union
and on Political Union, and which was also to provide the
trigger for the events which were to lead to Mrs Thatcher's
downfall, also marked the high point of Jacques Delors'
ambitions for rapid progress to ''European Union''. Thereafter events moved rapidly downhill. The British economy
had already moved into deep recession and the Continental countries were soon to follow. German unification,
embarked upon with high ambitions, great courage and
undue haste, was running into difficulties. The immense
drain upon the resources of the Western German economy
and the measures the Federal Government had to take to
counter the inflationary effects thus generated had serious
repercussions on the other Member States and hastened
their plunge into recession. Political difficulties in Denmark, with a coalition government balanced on a knife
edge, and in the United Kingdom, with a government with

a very narrow majority in Parliament and weakened by internal dissention, exacerbated the situation. Events in the Community, the emasculation of the policies laid down in the Rome Summit of October 1990 in the successive drafts under the Luxembourg and Netherlands Presidencies of what was to become the Maastricht Treaty, culminating in further watering down of the provisions at Maastricht itself including the opt outs for the United Kingdom on both Monetary Union and Social Policy, and the subsequent problems over ratification of the Treaty, all reflected these economic and political difficulties. In some ways it was a triumph that any Treaty, however inadequate, was signed and ratified at all.

The Maastricht Treaty was a natural sequel to the Single Act in the same way that the Single Act was a natural sequel to the Single Market. Nevertheless, my present purpose has simply been to write the story of the Single Market: the story of Maastricht and what lies beyond will need to come later. But there are two issues so bound up with the Single Market, yet so important in relation to the future, that they need to be addressed as part of the present study.

The first relates to timing. I have always taken the view that a Single Market would lead to a Single Currency and indeed that the full benefits of a Single Market could not be achieved without a Single Currency as indeed the history of the American economy illustrates: and that in time the Single Currency would lead to a Single Economy. I encapsulated this view in the statement I have already quoted, that the Single Market was not the end of the road but the road that led somewhere: and that "somewhere" was Economic Union. "Economic Union" was something I hoped, and expected, could be achieved in my lifetime and I would work for it: "Political Union", whatever that might mean, could not, and therefore I distanced myself from it. Herein lay the differences which emerged in the last days of the Commission of which I was a member between myself and Jacques Delors and most of the rest of the Commission. I regarded Economic Union as the objective we should fight for: Political Union was a battle for another day and there was no point in fighting tomorrow's battle before today's battle had been won. Jacques Delors and the rest of the Commission took the view that the two issues were inseperable: that the tide was running in our favour with the success of the Single Market Programme and we must seize the opportunity. For the time being they appeared to be right and they were to receive powerful support from Federal Chancellor Kohl who was to insist on Political Union as the *quid pro quo* for Germany accepting Monetary Union.

Underlying this difference in approach was an acute difference in the meaning attached to words, as was to come out very clearly in the negotiations leading up to the Maastricht Treaty and the subsequent disputes. "Federal" had been interpreted – or misinterpreted would be the better term – in the United Kingdom as the equivalent of that other figment of the imagination, the "Brussels Super State". Such an interpretation is alien, if not unintelligible, to the Continental mind and philosophy. Germany is a "Federal Republic" and the concept of "federation" is regarded as the cornerstone and guarantee of democracy. The United States takes much the same view. The introduction of the term "federal vocation" in the preamble of the draft Treaty was the handiwork of the Netherlands, one of the founder members of the Community and one of the oldest and most reputable of the world's democracies. And the tragedy of Yugoslavia flows directly from the breakdown of the federation. It is of particular interest that on his first official visit to Europe, President Clinton, in speaking to Young Europeans at Brussels on 9 January 1994, referred repeatedly to the need for "integration" in Europe.

> "The purpose of my trip to Europe" he said "is to help lead the movement to that integration and to assure you that America will be a strong partner in it."

And he went on to refer to:

> "a Europe that is integrated in terms of security, in terms of economics, in terms of democracies."

Clearly what he had in mind was the concept that on the Continent is known as "federation" – which after all is the American pattern, the American precedent and the American exemplar.

We find the same problem with the term "Political Union". "Political Union" does not mean political union in the sense that term would be used in the United Kingdom – indeed the term "United Kingdom" itself denotes a unitary state. In contrast, the term "Political Union" as used in the Maastricht Treaty means little more than a modest extension of the powers of the European Parliament, a step towards more democratic control of the Community institutions and a greater involvement of the ordinary citizens of Europe in the affairs of the Community *inter alia* by extending voting rights. Looked at in this way "Political Union" is simply reinforcing democracy by making governments, whether they operate through their own legislatures or through the Brussels institutions, more accountable to the people they represent. At a time when a widening gulf is opening up between governments and the people it is at least arguable that this is a move in the right direction.

There is another important, if somewhat complex, point to make in relation to "Political Union". The Maastricht Treaty is based on what is described as a "Three Pillar" approach. The First Pillar deals with matters of "Community competence". The Community can only act within the powers conferred by the Treaties, as amended in particular by the Single Act and now by those provisions of the Maastricht Treaty which constitute the First Pillar. Matters not covered by the Treaties are not matters of Community competence and cannot be dealt with by the Community as such. The long standing practice has been that such matters, if they are to be dealt with, are dealt with by "Intergovernmental Co-operation", that is the governments of the Member States work together outside the terms of the Treaties. The important difference is that while matters of Community competence are governed by the rules of the Treaties, particularly on questions of voting, the Commission's sole right of initiative applies, the Parliament is involved and the Court of Justice has jurisdiction, none of this applies to Intergovernmental Co-operation – here unanimity is the rule, the Commission is sidelined, the Parliament has no formal status and the Court of Justice is entirely excluded.

At the time of the Rome Summit in October 1990 it was contemplated that a wide range of such subjects, and particularly foreign policy and security, should be brought within Community competence. In the event, while they were included in the Maastricht Treaty it was only on an Intergovernmental basis and they constitute what are described as the Second and Third Pillars. The matters so covered are:

Title V – the Second Pillar – Common Foreign and Security Policy

Title VI – the Third Pillar – Justice and Home Affairs.

What used to be described as "Political Co-operation in the field of foreign policy" goes back to the 1970s; it appears as an important item in the Solemn Declaration in 1983: and it was given legal status in the Single Act in 1986. The Maastricht Treaty does not change the legal basis but it does add "security" although even that was foreshadowed by the Single Act: and now it also refers to "the eventual framing of a common defence policy which might in time lead to a common defence".

So far as justice and home affairs are concerned, these are matters which have also been dealt with for many years on an Intergovernmental basis in two groups, "Trevi" which deals with immigration, asylum and visas and "Pompidou" – organised by the Council of Europe in order to bring in some countries not in the Community – dealing with drugs and drug abuse. The Maastricht Treaty does add certain other matters hitherto dealt with through other channels such as international crime and international fraud.

There is not, and never has been, any bar to governments "co-operating" among themselves and as I have indicated they have done so in these very areas for very many years. What the Maastricht Treaty has done is to bring out into the open what governments have been doing in private and subject it to public scrutiny. That is wholly admirable. But there is little change in substance and to dignify it by the name of "Political Union" is to raise hopes on the one side and fears on the other neither of which is likely to be realised or to be justified.

In looking to the future my other point, and indeed concern, relates to the attitude of the United Kingdom, or perhaps more accurately of the UK Government, to the European Community, or the "European Union" as it now is.

I have described at some length and indeed analysed in Chapter 8 the particular difficulties which arose in the Thatcher years. But they were not difficulties which stemmed solely from Mrs Thatcher's own personality and views. Had it been so she would not have been able to sustain the attitude to Europe which she had adopted. On the contrary, her views reflected, albeit in an exaggerated way, the attitudes and outlook I described in my first chapter – attitudes which led to our standing aloof from the European Community for the first 25 years of its life. The task of statesmanship was to change these attitudes, to convince people that there was no going back to the 19th century, that we had to adapt ourselves, however painfully, to the 20th century, so that ultimately we could successfully enter the 21st century. Harold Macmillan tried and failed: through no fault of his own but through the intransigence of de Gaulle. Ted Heath appeared to have won: but it was merely the legal battle he won, not the battle for the whole hearted commitment of the British people. Mrs Thatcher displayed a split personality: on nationalistic grounds she was opposed to the whole concept of the Community: on economic grounds she realised that Britain must not be excluded from the increasingly dominant European market. She never resolved this dilemma and in the end it destroyed her.

The debates over the Maastricht Treaty have brought all these problems to the surface and exposed them to the light of day. The peculiarities of the British system of government has meant that a government with a slim majority ceased to be able to suppress dissent in its own ranks, and with an Opposition determined to exploit any difficulties in which the government found itself, irrespective of the merits, the stage was set for a major confrontation between the pro and anti-European elements. On paper the government survived with the narrowest possible margin. But in reality it was not like that at all. The anti-European faction in its own ranks was small: the Opposition was officially not only pro-European but more so than the government: and the truth of the matter really was that the government's difficulties flowed from an unholy alliance. But that of course is the way that politics works.

The bitter battles over the Maastricht Treaty were in a sense a blood letting, a catharsis. It had one wholly beneficial effect: it forced politicians, and to some extent the public, to face up to the situation, to try and understand what had happened over the last 40 years, to realise what commitments had been entered into and to ask themselves whether they wished to abide by the commitments their leaders had entered into on their behalf. In short, the time of obfuscation, of saying one thing and meaning another, has had to come to an end.

But the battles have also demonstrated how small the committed anti-European element is. Like all dissent it is capable of making a great deal of noise out of all proportion to its real support. It is well able in the present political climate to exercise an influence far greater than its numbers justify by exploiting divisions in its own party and opportunism on the part of the Opposition. In the case of Denmark, where a referendum meant that the precise state of public opinion could be analysed, the very narrow majority which emerged against the Treaty on the first referendum reflected a *de facto* coalition between those who opposed the Treaty on the ground that it went too far and those who opposed it on the ground that it did not go far enough. We had a similar situation in the United Kingdom where the only actual defeat the government suffered was the result of a coalition between a handful of

Conservative anti-Europeans and the official Opposition who felt that the Treaty did not go far enough because of the exclusion of the United Kingdom from the Social Chapter.

The critical next step will be the grand review in 1996 for which the Maastricht Treaty specifically provides. By then there will be a new President in France, possibly a new Federal Chancellor in Germany and almost certainly a General Election in the United Kingdom. We will by then almost certainly enter a new political era. At the same time Europe should be well on the road out of the recession which carries so heavy a responsibility for so much of our present troubles. It is just possible that we will see a repeat of what happened in the 1980s when the recovery from the recessions of the 1970s and the early 1980s led to 1985 and the launch of the Single Market Programme. History does not repeat itself but there are parallels between one era and another. But these are issues we will need to examine in greater detail when we come to carry the story of the Single Market forward to Maastricht and beyond.

*Appendices*

# European Union forward from the Single Market Programme and "1992"

**Address by The Rt Hon The Lord Cockfield
European University Institute – Florence,
12 October 1989**

## A turning point in history

There are turning points in history. Frequently only dimly perceived at the time but later clearly identified. The renaissance of the Community which was launched by the Internal Market Programme and, in its wake, the Single European Act is likely to prove such a turning point.

The roots of change often go back a very long way. Nevertheless a point is reached when the process of change suddenly seems to take off. Thus when the British Prime Minister quotes Magna Carta as having preceded the Declaration of the Rights of Man by several centuries she is entirely right: but this does not alter the fact that the French revolution changed the world in a way that Runnymede never did.

# The birth of the concept of European Union

Over the centuries, repeated attempts were made to unify Europe by force – the Romans, Charlemagne, Napoleon and, in our own day, Hitler. They all ultimately failed. What distinguishes the present move to European Union is that it is based on free and voluntary agreement not undertaken in war or under the duress of war. In that it is not unique – the federations in both Canada and Australia were also the product of voluntary agreement, although in those cases the circumstances were much easier as there was not, except to a limited extent, the same history of conflict between the participants.

The concept of European Union was firmly embedded in the founding treaties, the Treaty of Paris and the Treaty of Rome. But after a vigorous and successful start the Community ran into serious difficulties. First with de Gaulle, reflecting his intensely nationalistic approach, and then more insidiously but possibly more damagingly by the onset of the recession and the enlargement of the Community to include new Member States who – events were to show – did not all entirely share the visions of the founders of the Community.

# The Internal Market Programme and the Single European Act

But as Europe gradually recovered from the recession, the original vision of a united Europe began to emerge once again. In 1983 the Solemn Declaration on European Union was subscribed to at Stuttgart by the Heads of Government and the Foreign Ministers of all the Member States. At this stage sceptics could still claim, in the way that some countries still try to dismiss what they do not like, that this was mere rhetoric. But in June 1985 we produced the White Paper on the Completion of the Internal Market. This was endorsed by the Heads of Government when they met at Milan the same month. And within a matter of months this in turn was followed by the negotiation of the Single European Act at Luxembourg in December 1985.

The Single Act both gave legislative backing to the Internal Market Programme in the clearest and most specific terms, and it enacted substantial improvements in procedures to ensure that the goal was achieved. But the Single Act did more than this. It provided also for the implementation of many of the policies set out in the Solemn Declaration. From time to time we need to remind ourselves of just what a tremendous canvas was painted by the Single Act:

The Internal Market;
Social Policy;
Economic and Monetary Union;
Economic and Social Cohesion;
Science and Technology;
The Environment, and
Political Co-operation in the sphere of foreign policy.

So, suddenly we had passed from rhetoric to action. The vision was no longer just a vision: it was a vision in action. This is why these events of 1985 were, and will prove to be, a turning point in history. Interestingly, the date likely to be associated with these dramatic events is likely not to be 1985 but 1992, the date set for the completion of the Internal Market Programme and which is now part not only of the history of the Community but also of popular parlance.

## From the Internal Market Programme to European Union

The seminal importance of the Internal Market Programme is that it initiated a process of change. It has demonstrated that the will is master of events and that if the will is there the events can be moulded in the form we want. It started a whole process of change; and when the Heads of Government at Hannover in

June of last year declared that the process was "irreversible" they were setting their seal of approval on far more than the Internal Market Programme. And so events are unfolding themselves. Monetary Union we will have in a matter of a few years: and Economic Union will follow. We need have no doubt now that we will see European Union in both the economic and political sense, and it will be achieved within the lifetime of many alive today. The time when one could stop it is passed. The turning point was marked perhaps by the British Prime Minister's Bruges speech: a speech which was designed to attack the whole concept of European Union ended up by calling forth the forces supporting European Union, uniting them and giving them fresh determination. *If you toll the bell, beware, it may toll for thee.*

## The issues we now face

So the questions we now have to ask ourselves are these:

What will be the shape of this economic and political union?
Who will participate in it?
What will be its implications for the world outside the Community both in political and economic terms?

The great merit of the establishment of the Jean Monnet chair in the European University Institute is that it provides a forum at which these issues can be debated: in which ideas can be tossed into the arena and progress made in the cut and thrust of debate. On the present occasion, I can do no more than suggest the lines our future consideration should take and leave it to subsequent discussion and study to flesh out the ideas, to develop them, to endorse or even to reject.

But the bed-rock on which we stand is this. In the 1992 Programme, and in the Single Act, we have started a process that will not, and cannot, be stopped. Our task is to mould that process to the greater benefit of the people of Europe: not of the Community alone but of Europe as a whole.

# The future structure of Europe

In a number of speeches I have delivered in the last year or so, particularly in the address I gave at the Swiss Institute of International Affairs in Zurich in October of last year and in the "Mobile" lecture I delivered at the London School of Economics in June of this year, I set out the way that I thought the Community would develop in the years ahead. I do not propose repeating the arguments I then deployed: but the broad conclusions I then came to, I adhere to. Indeed subsequent events have moved in a direction consistent with, not opposed to, the analysis I had set out.

No longer can we simply look at the Community in isolation. Not only are other countries applying, or contemplating applying for membership, but the relationship with the EFTA countries is developing more vigorously than at any time since the Luxembourg Declaration of 1984 set out the concept of the "European Economic Space". Of critical importance also is that we are now seeing the gradual demise of the Russian Empire. Nothing like that has occurred since the decline and fall of the Roman Empire a thousand years or more ago. This is leaving a vacuum in Europe which must be filled, and it must be filled I suggest by Europe. It has another important consequence, namely that the prospect of military conflict which dominated the policies of the Super Powers for so many years is fading. As it fades the economic dimension becomes more and more important. It is therefore the European Community with its roots firmly bedded in Economic Union which needs to play the lead role in these future developments. I return to these matters later in this address.

So it is the future structure of Europe as a whole we are now compelled to look at: the way the Community strictly defined will develop, and what the relationships will be between that Community and the structure which will emerge in the Greater Europe. The position is greatly complicated by the fact that the Community itself is in a process of rapid development. There is no doubt that that development will go ahead and succeed, but there is serious doubt whether all the members of the Community will go along with those developments.

In the previous lectures to which I have referred, I identified four potential groupings. First, what one might describe as an inner circle of those members of the Community who would progress to full Economic and Political Union. Second, a group of countries – some present members of the Community but possibly some others as well – who would accept Economic but not Political Union. Third, a group – again possibly including some present members of the Community but mainly countries at present outside the Community – who would accept something like the 1992 Programme but no more. And finally an outer circle comprising a free trade area but no more.

At first sight such a pattern would appear to be excessively complex. But in fact it is no more complex than the situation which exists at present, with the EFTA countries forming a free trade area with the Community, with many countries with varying association agreement with the Community, and the Community itself divided by special arrangements and derogations to meet the difficulties or prejudices of particular Member States. Indeed it could well be regarded as a rationalization of a situation which in fact already exists.

Nevertheless, my own view is that countries would tend to gravitate towards one end of the spectrum or the other. There are strong practical – let alone political – reasons making this likely to happen. The institutional problems of getting a four tier structure to operate, and even more so to develop, are likely to push strongly in this direction. We can already see these forces at work in the Community/EFTA relationship where – even with what still remains essentially a free trade relationship – there is acute dissatisfaction on the part of the EFTA countries at their exclusion from the decision-making process and a determination on the part of the Community that its autonomy in decision making should not be put at risk by the Community/

EFTA relationship. The fact that final agreement on the convention on non-life insurance between the Community and Switzerland was held up for so long reflected fears on both sides that their future independence in decision making was put at risk.

The issues involved are interrelated and interdependent. The number of groups, or tiers, will depend on how flexible the countries comprising them are, and this in turn depends on who those countries are. Some countries regard the common good of the Community as the overriding objective. Others are determined to defend their undiluted national sovereignity to the last gasp. Countries with a tradition of neutrality may not find this easily reconciled with the growing competence of the Community, and the more we extend our ambitions to cover the wider Europe, the greater the problem of finding an acceptable accord between different political philosophies.

One cannot carry this sort of discussion very far before it becomes necessary to talk in terms of the likely outlook and political stance of individual countries. Here one is beginning to tread on delicate ground. It is all too easy to upset the political sensitivities of particular countries. Nor is the position made any easier by the fact that statements or declarations by the governments of individual countries often need to be taken with a pinch of salt. A declaration of intent to die in the last ditch may be no more than a cover for retreat, and a rigid and intransigent stance may be essentially a bargaining ploy. Nor must we entirely discount the fact that governments, like individuals, do sometimes learn from experience, and they may at the last moment come to the conclusion that it is better not to jump into the abyss after all. So far as we are concerned, therefore, we have to divine what is likely to happen under the pressure of events: not even what we ourselves would want to happen or others would express a determination to ensure should not happen, but what we believe at the end of the day *will* happen.

# Political Union

I believe – and certainly in Europe this view is widespread – that Political Union will come. I believe equally that it is a mistake to talk in terms of a "United States of Europe" as this suggests that we should – or would – follow the American pattern. Not only do I believe this unlikely – essentially on the ground that the United States gives far more power to the federal authority than is likely to be necessary or acceptable in Europe – but because the comparison is likely to arouse unnecessary and ill informed opposition. I will return to the question of the powers and institutions of a Political Union in a moment, but at this stage I would emphasise that both the extent of the powers and the nature of the institutions are as of now completely open questions. With these reservations clearly in mind, I would suggest that the kernel of Political Union lies in the close and growing co-operation between France and Germany – the Franco-German axis as it is sometimes called. This is not new. In the past it has waxed and waned, but in recent years, particularly under the leadership of President Mitterand and Chancellor Kohl, it has become the dominant force in the Community – strengthened, I regret to say, by the withdrawal of my own country to the sidelines of European development. Once France and Germany moved decisively towards Political Union they would be likely – not least for economic and strategic reasons – to carry the Benelux countries – Belgium, Holland and Luxembourg – with them. Nor would Italy, with its firm commitment to the European ideal, be left behind. So we would see at long last emerging the objective the Treaty of Rome originally looked ahead to; and embracing, understandably, the original, founder members of the Community. Once this development was underway, one would expect both Ireland and Spain, who have both shown a strong European commitment, to join in: and possibly Portugal too. Of the present Community this would leave out only the United Kingdom, Denmark and Greece. However much I regret having to say so, I see no reasonable prospect of the first two being prepared to take such a historic step forward: and on Greece I can express no opinion.

## "The European Union"

Interestingly, what has emerged from this brief survey corresponds very closely to the pattern which emerged when the decision was taken in 1985 to set up the Intergovernmental Conference at Luxembourg. The real significance is that what happened then and what has happened since – and is likely to be repeated when the time comes to decide on the Intergovernmental Conference on Economic and Monetary Union – establishes very clearly the position that, when the chips are down, the great majority of Member States will go along with the ultimate development of the Community to full Economic and Political Union. I suggest that we call this full Political and Economic Union quite simply "The European Union", thus reflecting the terminology of the Solemn Declaration, and that we eschew descriptions such as "the United States of Europe".

Those who choose not to go along will simply be left behind. President Mitterand, in a recent speech, made precisely this point. There is now no question of a minority preventing the majority going forward. Something else follows from this analysis. The "minority" is likely to be too small and too lacking in cohesion to form a viable group. Consequently a "two speed Europe" in the sense hitherto understood is neither a serious threat nor a serious possibility. This I regard as a point of major importance.

## The Greater Europe

Given therefore that we have in "the European Union" a tightly knit and cohesive Community, even if somewhat smaller than at present, what we now have to consider is what will be the structure of the Greater Europe – East and West – as we move towards and into the 21st century: and what will be the relationship between the European Union and the other elements in the structure which will be necessary to embrace the Greater Europe.

At this point we need to go to the other end of the spectrum. The position of East Germany raises particular problems and I would only stress that this is a matter best dealt with under the umbrella of the European Community. But leaving this on one side, there is no reasonable prospect that in the foreseeable future the countries of Eastern Europe will join or be able to join an Economic and Political Union with the countries of Western Europe. Indeed the most that can be contemplated at least as a first step – the significance of this qualification I explain later – would be the creation of a free trade area, such as exists at present between the EFTA countries and the Community. A free trade area involves no derogation from sovereignty and is compatible with complete and continuing independence in the political field. Free trade areas exist outside Europe – recent examples are the US/Canada Free Trade Agreement and a similar accord between Australia and New Zealand. In principle, such a development gives rise to no insuperable problem, although the detail can be fraught with difficulty. But a "free trade area" does not in any sense constitute a form of Community membership. This – and its implications – need to be clearly understood.

The European Community itself is not, and never has been, simply a free trade area. There is much misunderstanding on this point, particularly in my own country, and the position therefore needs to be made crystal clear.

The Community started as a customs union – but in case this gives too narrow a view perhaps it would be better to say that the Customs Union was the foundation stone of the Community. A customs union requires a common external tariff and a common external trade policy. The powers for this purpose must be vested in a supra-national body. Consequently, the Community started life with the Member States transferring their sovereignty to the Community in one of the most sensitive of all fields, namely fiscal policy, a matter which seems to be overlooked by latter-day defenders of national sovereignty. It is of the essence of a customs union that once goods have lawfully entered the territory of the customs union they are entitled to freedom of circulation throughout the whole territory of the customs union, thus avoiding many of the troubles and complications of a free trade area. It also follows from this that the freedom of movement of goods is an essential corollary of the freedom of circulation that the customs union is designed to achieve.

The EFTA countries are no longer satisfied with the conventional type of free trade agreement. Quite apart from the difficulties – not just administrative but economic as well – that rules of origin give rise to, there is the feeling that the "weaker" partner, in this case the EFTA countries, are having rules imposed on them that they have no say in the formulation: there is the feeling too that the benefits of free trade should not be confined to goods but should extend also to services, that market opening measures taken by the Community should be extended to the EFTA countries, and so on. The close physical proximity of the EFTA countries to the Community countries and the close trading relationships give added force to these feelings. As I mentioned earlier, in 1984 a declaration was signed by the Community and the EFTA countries at Luxembourg which provided for the creation of a "European Economic Space". Since then, much effort has been deployed to making this a reality, although to be frank there has been more effort than result. Currently there is much discussion among the EFTA countries themselves about their future relationship with the Community: one country – Austria – has already applied for membership, others may follow. There is talk also of a customs union to replace the present free trade agreement.

All this has to be judged against a background in which the Community itself is developing rapidly. If the Community – or the greater part of it – develops into a full-blown Economic and Political Union, this may mean that membership is no longer a feasible option for countries that might otherwise have wished to join.

We have therefore a situation where, at one extreme there would be a full Political and Economic Union embracing probably fewer than the present 12 Member States, and at the other extreme a simple, traditional free trade area. What can we put in between to accommodate those European states which want more than a simple free trade relationship but are not prepared or able to accept full Political and Economic Union?

Precisely what form the new structure would take in the case of these countries will, I believe, largely be dictated by negotiation between the EFTA countries and the Community, influenced in greater or less degree by the handful of Community countries unable to go with full Political and Economic Union. It is relevant that the two most important countries which might fall into this last group were themselves originally members of EFTA.

The most promising form this new relationship would take would be an extended Customs Union embracing services as well as goods. Services, of course, are not normally subject to customs duties but the cardinal feature of a customs union, namely the freedom of circulation within the territory of the customs union, is critically important in the case of services.

In short, the structure which emerged on the basis of this approach would be very close to the core of the "1992" Programme shorn of some of its more contentious aspects. Such an extended Customs Union would need in one way or another to accommodate agricultural products as well. There are various ways this could be done, the simplest from the technical point of view being that the members of the union would follow the prices set by the CAP but costs would fall directly on the countries concerned.

## The pattern of the Greater Europe

A European structure of this sort – namely "the European Union" embracing most but not all of the present members of the Community, an extended Customs Union embracing a further group of countries closely associated with the European Union, mainly the EFTA countries plus those of the present Community membership not joining the European Union, and a free trade area bringing in the rest, or virtually the rest, of Europe – is a logical development of the trends which are already apparent. It has the added virtue of being stable, coherent and flexible. It offers, too, the prospect of further development. Countries could, if they so wished, and agreement was forthcoming, progress from the free trade area to the Customs Union or from the Customs Union to membership of the full European Union.

## The institutional aspects

I have not touched upon the institutional aspects of such a Europe-wide structure. To do so would entail an impossibly long extension of this lecture, and it is also likely to prove the most difficult and the most contentious part of the whole exercise. It is not just the question of the transfer or merger or sovereignty. The most sensitive point is "to whom?". Interestingly, this proved one of the most difficult points in the negotiation of the American Constitution. In our own case, the European Parliament has already staked out its claim. It will be strongly resisted by some Member States particularly where, as in the United Kingdom, the European Parliament has been kept very much at arm's length. In many of the Continental countries where there is "freedom of movement" between national Parliaments and the European Parliament, the transfer would not be regarded as so outrageous. I suspect in the end some compromise formula will be found – as indeed it was in the US – with the adoption of a bicameral system, the upper house effectively representing the Member States as Mr Michael Heseltine has suggested. But this in turn raises the further problem whether that upper house should be elected, or non-elected as the present Council of Ministers is – and indeed the House of Lords in my own country. And critically, also, the powers of this "upper house" in relation to the "lower house".

Although it may sound surprising to say so, to some degree I regard this discussion at this stage as academic. "Political Union" will be achieved by means of a number of steps in separate areas – many of these areas constitute parts of Economic and Monetary Union, but to these will be added foreign policy, which to some extent is already covered by political co-operation, defence, internal security and ultimately, I suspect, basic social security provisions. The institutions needed for these developments will evolve, to a large degree *ad hoc*, but they and the experience they generate will contribute to, and indeed will point to the way forward. I think this kind of evolutionary development is much more likely – and much more likely to succeed – than any attempt at this stage to produce a "grand design".

What I have said reflects my own, somewhat cautious approach to these fundamental issues. But there is always the possibility that we may see a re-run of what happened with the Messina Conference and the Treaty of Rome, namely a sudden emergence of a determination to have done with the talking and get on with the action. The Treaty of Rome set out the principles and provided a "transitional period" of 12 years for the detail to be thrashed out. In other words, the "step by step" approach took place after the Treaty was signed not before. Perhaps in the end that is how you do make progress.

## Political and economic implications

The political strength of the European Union, embracing 250 million people or more, would be absolutely immense. Moreover, it would be backed by an economic area, joined to it by a customs union or free trade area making it by far and away the biggest and most powerful economic entity in the world. The European Union would thus take its place as one of the three or four Super Powers of the world.

This, of course, is "potential". The part actually played by the European Union would depend on the cohesiveness of its constituent parts, on the extent to which it was able to mobilise the strength of the whole economic area of which it formed the most influential part, and on the policies it developed towards the outside world. Neither China nor India are the political or economic forces that either their population or potential would justify, whether this is by choice or by an inability to develop that potential. Nor does Japan play the role its economic strength would justify, although it is now somewhat hesitatingly beginning to emerge from the wings of the stage.

The European Union, because of its long democratic traditions, its culture, and its approach to human problems, would be a great liberalising influence in the world.

The economic consequences are much more obvious and much more urgent. Whatever happens we must try and avoid the absurdites of the "Fortress Europe" campaign waged by elements in America and Japan. Based as it was on confusion, misunderstanding and to some degree misrepresentation, it achieved nothing other than to create suspicion and make co-operation in solving the inevitable problems of change more difficult. The European Community has always been a powerful force for liberalism in world trade. I would expect its greater and more powerful successor to be the same. Certainly it would be very much in its own interest to be so.

## Conclusion

It is, I think, important to ask ourselves what is the motivation behind the development of the European Union and the restructuring of relationships in Europe as a whole.

Politics is the pursuit of power. One can see this in its most naked form in the case of the Super Powers, the United States and Russia. Each in their own way was seeking world domination, although both would probably each in their own way express it somewhat differently. But since Vietnam, the political ambitions of the United States have lost momentum: and economic problems have given impetus to this change in emphasis. Russia, too, has been faced with a situation which would have been inconceivable even a few years ago, with massive internal dissent, the growth of nationalism and the clear determination of most of the conquerred territories in Europe to regain their independence. We already see both the United States and Russia turning in upon themselves. The vacuum thus left – and it is essentially a European vacuum – must be filled, and I hope and believe it will be filled, by Europe itself and in a new and restructured form. Russia in particular is an Asiatic power, not a European one: and she has no real place in Europe. This is not to deny the importance of Russia, but she is neither entitled to a dominant voice in Europe nor is it in her own interests to seek to exercise such a domination. The motivation of such a new Europe will not be essentially a global political motive. Europe will take its place as a Super Power but it will not do so with global politics either as its driving force or as its outcome.

We are, I hope and trust, eternally grateful to the American people for the massive contribution they made to the restructuring of Europe after the war: and for the defence they provided against the Russians in their days of aggression. But times have changed and we must change with them. It is a different world and it demands different policies.

The objective of the original Treaties was the preservation of the peace; and because economic rivalry was so often the root cause of war, the Treaties set out to achieve the objective through Economic Union. That, in my view, remains the correct objective and the correct path to its achievement. If we look forward not just to the European Union, but in time to a greater European Union embracing all the countries of Europe, both the objective and the path must be primarily an economic one. If peace can best be secured by prosperity, then it is prosperity we must create.

Very rarely has mankind been offered such an opportunity. There are many people who would regard this pursuit of peace based on prosperity as "idealistic", the term having a pejorative connotation. But that is a superficial view. What has happened in the world is that warfare between the Great Powers is no longer a feasible option. There will be wars between lesser powers, as we have seen in recent years, and from time to time the Great Powers will get involved, directly or indirectly. But so far as the Great Powers themselves are concerned, the struggle for influence and power will be an economic one and a philosophical one. This is the scenario to which we must now turn our minds and this is the basis on which we must draw up our plans for Europe's development. In short it is the European Community which now moves centre stage. The responsibility falls on us: and we must shoulder our responsibilities.

I have, in this lecture, set out the basis on which that development should take place to achieve the objectives we want to attain. It is a perfectly feasible scenario based on both history and the needs of our times. As I have said, it is stable but flexible: it provides room for development. It is evolutionary, not revolutionary. Above all, it reflects the aspirations of the European people. We have reached the stage where visions need to be translated into reality. What we now need are the statesmen to seize the opportunities, guide the development and turn the vision into reality.

# Postscript

This speech was delivered last October (1989) before events in Eastern Europe had achieved their present momentum. But the analysis set out in the lecture is still entirely valid and, if anything, the new architecture suggested for the "Greater Europe" – a strong and united Community as the lynchpin, with an extended Customs Union covering services as well as goods associated with it, and a free trade area covering the rest of the Greater Europe – is now already taking shape before our very eyes. The negotiations between the Community and the EFTA countries to achieve the "European Economic Space", in which there would be freedom of movement of goods, services, people and capital, are now pressing ahead and trade and co-operation agreements with most of the countries of Eastern Europe have been signed or are in course of negotiation.

Just occasionally in human history a window of opportunity opens. When it does – and it now has – we must take our courage in our hands and seize the opportunity.

*20 March 1990*

*1992 – Bilan d'une renaissance*
# Le Programme 92: Objectifs et méthodes

## Address by The Rt Hon The Lord Cockfield Séance Académique – Brussels, 17 December 1992

"Atmosphere" is something which is difficult to recreate and often only dimly remembered. It is a matter of the spirit, not of the mind. Not for historians or even philosophers but possibly for poets. It is easy enough to produce a catalogue of events or a list of names. But to recreate the atmosphere that gave birth to these events and inspired the people whose names we remember is an entirely different matter. But unless we try, unless we understand however remotely and imperfectly what that atmosphere was we will never really understand the events. And events which mark a turning point in the history of the Community as the Single Market Programme did deserve more than a mere recital of facts and figures or indeed the names of the players of the game.

In these dark and troubled times it is not easy to recall the atmosphere that existed in the summer and autumn of 1984 when the first Commission presided over by Jacques Delors was taking shape. It was almost a Golden Age. After all, when Thatcher and Mitterrand were in close accord and in the United Kingdom Jacques Delors was held in high esteem as one of the most distinguished Finance Ministers of his time, this indeed must have been a Golden Age. It was the period I had in mind when in a speech in the House of Lords the day after Mrs Thatcher's downfall I referred to: "the happier times of years gone by".

The first awakening came in the early 1980s notably with the Solemn Declaration on European Union which was signed in June 1983 at Stuttgart by the Heads of Government and their Foreign Ministers. The following year, in June 1984, the Fontainebleau Summit under the French Presidency solved all the outstanding problems which had dogged the Community for so many years – the Common Agricultural Policy, own resources, budget discipline and the British budget contribution. There is something depressingly familiar about this catalogue of woes and before many years had passed these problems were to return to haunt us. But for the moment all was sweetness and light. A window of opportunity had opened. And it was through this window we went. The way was clear to relaunch the Community. And the Single Market Programme was to emerge as the flagship of that enterprise. And if I may be forgiven a personal note, it was to prove my last and most enduring achievement. When now eight years on I look once again at the photographs of the new Commission which were taken at Royaumont in December 1984 we looked full of enthusiasm, energy and hope. Whatever the calendar might say, it was the springtime of our youth and of the Community.

You may feel that this is a diversion from the hard facts of who did what and why. You would be wrong to take that view. The success of the programme was a triumph of the spirit over the lethargy and narrow vision of the past. Unless you understand that you will never understand why the programme succeeded over what were regarded as insuperable odds. Why we are here today to celebrate victory in times otherwise clouded by doubt and uncertainty.

In these more troubled days when reputations can so often be clouded by unjustified criticism may I say that the complete and total trust invested in me by Jacques Delors, his clarity of vision and unfailing support were a major factor in the success of my own endeavours.

The broad concept of the Single Market, the freedom of movement of goods, of people, of services and of capital was an integral part of the Treaty of Rome itself. In the early days rapid progress was made: the Customs Union, the foundation stone of the Community, was completed ahead of time and the Community turned its hand to dealing with the non-tariff barriers. But in the 1970s progress ground to a halt due not least to the double recession which struck the world following the two great oil price increases. As we moved into the 1980s and the world recovered from the recession, there was a growing awareness in the Community of how much ground we had lost compared with our competitors elsewhere in the industrial world and notably in the United States and Japan. So the concept of relaunching the Community emerged and nowhere did it receive greater support than in the top ranks of European industry and one remembers in particular the names of Wisse Dekker, Jacques Solvay and Pehr Gyllenhammar.

In 1982 the Heads of Government meeting at Copenhagen called on the Council: "to decide . . . on the priority measures proposed by the Commission to reinforce the internal market".

In some ways the significant part of this quotation, if read carefully, is that it recognises that as always the initiative had come from the Commission.

The following January (1983) the Internal Market Council was set up. (The term used in the Community was always the "Internal Market": but in the United Kingdom it is more usual now to refer to the "Single Market". The terms are of course interchangeable.) I was at that time the Senior Trade Minister in London and responsible at Cabinet level for the operations of the Council. So my connection with the Internal Market preceded my coming to Brussels and this was to stand me in good stead when I joined the

Commission. But in those early days the Council acquired no high profile and although it did valuable work, and a notable contribution was made by Karl-Heinz Narjes, the Commissioner then responsible, the Council created no very great stir. Interestingly in the Solemn Declaration on European Union to which I have already referred, the Internal Market did not appear until page 14 of the English translation: it came only after a long list of other policies – Economic Strategy: the EMS: Economic and Monetary Union: Economic Cohesion: External Relations: and the Developing Countries: the text refers only to the "remaining obstacles" as though much progress had been made and the obstacles remaining were few in number. The following year, the Fontainebleau Summit in June 1984, one of the most important meetings in the history of the Community, did not refer to the Internal Market at all.

What was it then that suddenly propelled the Internal Market Programme from the humble position it had occupied in the Solemn Declaration to the lead position it was soon to occupy and its ultimate emergence as one of the Community's great achievements? The key I think lies in the publication in June 1985 of the White Paper on the Completion of the Internal Market. The decision to publish a "White Paper" followed British precedent. To others in the Community the term and indeed the very concept of a "White Paper" was novel. It was translated in the French as "*Livre Blanc*" and then re-translated back into English as "White Book" and in the Continental Europe is still commonly referred to as the "White Book".

The cardinal features of the White Paper which caught the imagination were these:

*First* that it was a complete programme: not a bit here and a bit there, not the choice of "priorities" or measures favoured by particular Member States but the whole job "completely and effectively": to use the words which were to appear in the Conclusions of the Milan Summit: there was, I said, only one "priority" and that was to do the complete job.

*Second* the programme was set in a time frame: not just "1992" for the programme as a whole, but every single one of the original 300 proposals had its own timetable.

A subtle change, originally of presentation but ultimately of substance, also took place. The original concept of the Internal Market was simply one of removing non-tariff barriers and the work done hitherto was conceived in that context. We now began to talk about a Europe without frontiers. This concept of removing the frontiers and the controls which went with them was to form the hallmark of the new approach to the Internal Market. It underlay the structure of the White Paper Programme which was directed to removing the *barriers* whether they were physical barriers, technical barriers or fiscal barriers. And in due time it was to be reflected in the Single European Act which defines the Internal Market as:

> ". . . an area without internal frontiers in which the freedom of movement of goods, persons, services and capital is ensured . . .".

For the first time also it brought home to my own government in the United Kingdom that "Completing the Internal Market" of necessity went much further than they had imagined and therein lay the seeds of my disagreement with many of my former colleagues in that government.

It was one thing to draw up the programme, if it was to succeed it was also essential to put in a discipline. This took the form primarily of an Annual Report. Interestingly originally this was promised in response to repeated calls from the European Parliament for information but it was to serve an even more important role. The Annual Report not only enabled progress to be monitored but it also identified who was responsible for any failure to meet the target whether it was Council, Parliament or the Commission itself. In due time further provision was made in the Single European Act for a Report to the Heads of Government at the half way stage – *i.e.* before the end of 1988 – a further report in 1990 and a Final Report before the end of 1992 all designed to ensure that progress was maintained and momentum was not lost.

But there was another factor as well. The White Paper was produced on 14 June 1985, less than five and a half months after we, as a new Commission, had taken up duty on 6 January. This quite remarkable turn of speed – many of the other major programmes to which the Commission had committed itself did not appear for a matter of years – meant that when the Heads of Government met at Milan a few days later they had before them the concrete expression of the desire to "relaunch the Community", a programme which for sheer breadth and depth caught the imagination. The White Paper was no mere catalogue of proposals, it also set out a clear philosophy. It built upon old ideas and developed new ideas. It set out the "New Approach to Standards" as the model for future Community legislation: and extended the concept from goods to services and particularly the financial services. It developed the intellectual argument for linking success in the Single Market to progress in the structural funds and what in these days is called 'cohesion". We had entered a new world: it was no longer talk but detailed plans for action: no longer the rhetoric but the promise of achievement. The Heads of Government rose to the occasion: they not only endorsed the programme but underlined the sense of urgency and determination by adding to the date of 31 December 1992 the words "at the latest".

I am supposed to talk to you about "*méthodes*". It is only right therefore that I should say how this remarkable turn of speed was achieved. We were able, of course, to draw upon an immense amount of work already done in the Commission Services. Thus no less than 100 of the 300 proposals set out in the White Paper had already been tabled: that is they were already with the Council and the Parliament, although to be brutal I often wished subsequently that I had been able to start with a completely blank sheet: it is often more difficult to deal with proposals encrusted with barnacles than to have to start afresh. The imaginative scope of the White Paper approach also inspired the Commission Services who felt that at long last they had a clear lead and knew exactly what was expected of them. I cannot praise too highly the work done by the Director Generals involved and their staff and particularly Fernand Braun, Paolo Cecchini, Riccardo Perissich and Peter Klein.

But there was another factor. My decision to accept the offer to join the Commission was on the basis that I should take responsibility for the Internal Market and this was agreed with Jacques Delors, who was then President-designate, at the outset. In the subsequent negotiations leading up to the allocation of specific portfolios I put it to President Delors that if I was to make a success of the job it was essential that I should have control not just of the traditional Internal Market portfolio but also of those elements which would have to be an integral part of the kind of "complete" programme I had in mind. With his strong support I acquired, in addition to the Internal Market portfolio, the Financial Services, Company Law and Taxation, the Customs Union and Indirect Taxation as well as the lead on those industries with a particularly close link with the Internal Market, namely food manufacture, the pharmaceutical and chemical industries, construction and wholesale and retail distribution. This avoided a great deal of argument and negotiation which otherwise would have been inevitable had these matters been in the hands of other Commissioners. Some major portfolios which while important in relation to the Single Market also raised much wider issues, for example, Competition Policy and Transport, very properly were the prerogative of other Commissioners. But here and elsewhere my own Chef de Cabinet, Adrian Fortescue, who had had a long association with the Community both as a member of Christopher Soames' *Cabinet* when we first joined the Community and in the Diplomatic Service and had an extensive knowledge of how the Community operated, played an invaluable role. He was supported by a *Cabinet* of exception quality and he was able to maintain the closest links with the Chefs de Cabinet of other Commissioners involved, or indeed interested, which meant that much of the work was able to go to the Commission on an agreed basis. This in turn meant that the Commission itself could concentrate its attention on the policy issues involved knowing that the detail had already been examined, discussed and agreed. In this way we adopted a procedure not unlike that which enables business in Cabinet in the United Kingdom to be transacted so expeditiously: there the existence of Cabinet Committees where much of the detailed work is done means that Cabinet itself can concentrate on the issues of policy.

The endorsement by the Heads of Government at Milan was the first and indeed a massive step forward. But a second step was needed to ensure the success of the programme. "Unanimity" lay at the heart of paralysis of Community action as it meant that a single Member State could block progress on which all others were agreed, often for narrow national or even sectoral interests. It is too little realised how often opposition in the Council of Ministers does not represent a considered opinion by the government of the country in question but an attempt by individual Ministers or even officials to defend their own cabbage patch. The Treaty itself provided that in general after the "transitional period" decision should be by qualified majority vote and save in certain specific areas, of which Article 100 dealing with harmonization was one of the most important, unanimity would have withered away. Unfortunately as a result of the Luxembourg Compromise, the legality of which is much open to question, the Council of Ministers insisted on unanimity on virtually everything whether the Treaty so required or not with the result that progress ground to a halt. It was clear that if the Single Market Programme were to be completed as the Heads of Government had demanded something had to be done to ensure that, at least on Internal Market matters, majority voting prevailed. The instrument which came to hand was the Single European Act.

The Single Act had a dual provenance. In part its inspiration was the Solemn Declaration and a determination on the part of Jacques Delors with the vigorous support of Lorenzo Natali to give effect to "European Union" and the policies underlying it.

In part it was to introduce majority voting for the Single Market and to involve the European Parliament through the co-operation procedure. There is no doubt that but for this change in procedure there would have been no prospect of the Single Market Programme succeeding. In presentational and indeed psychological terms, the Single Act made another change. While in the Solemn Declaration the Single Market had appeared in the list of policies at the very end of the line, it now appeared in pole position. While in origin this could be said to be a matter of logical arrangement of the draft, it confirmed the emergence of the Single Market as occupying the lead position.

To be perfectly frank I was apprehensive about the increased involvement of the European Parliament. Experience in the House of Lords had taught me how time consuming detailed work on legislation could be: I had my hands full in dealing with the Council of Ministers and I did not relish having this work duplicated in the Parliament. The Parliament was equally dissatisfied, feeling that the new role it was given was totally inadequate. In the event we were both proved wrong. The Parliament was able to make a very significant contribution in improving the quality of the legislation: most of the changes it made were accepted by the Commission and a large proportion adopted by the Council. So in the end we all gained. Throughout, the Parliament and particularly the Kangaroo Group led by Boz Ferranti were a powerful force pressing for the abolition of the frontiers and frontier controls. And on a personal note I may say that the support the Parliament gave me in this and other matters was invaluable and many of the friendships I then made have endured.

One of the more remarkable but unsung achievements of the introduction of majority voting was that very rarely was voting actually resorted to. Once the Presidency observed that a majority had emerged, the proposition would be approved without the need for a formal vote and without therefore a minority being identified and isolated.

There was one other significant improvement made in working methods. Following the endorsement of the White Paper Programme at the Milan Summit, the Luxembourg Presidency which had taken over from the Italian introduced a rolling programme system for the Council of Ministers on a troika basis. The agenda for Council meetings is set by the Presidency but as a Presidency lasts only for six months what was happening was that the incumbent Presidency would set its own priorities but six months was too short a period for much success to be achieved: the incoming Presidency would have its own priorities and tended then to shelve what its predecessor had done: so much was started and so little finished. The system introduced by Luxembourg envisaged a rolling programme agreed between the sitting (or outgoing) Presidency, the incoming Presidency and the one after that. The programme would then be updated by each successive Presidency. This introduced a continuity in the work and it contributed very significantly to the efficiency of operation of the Council.

It is worth mentioning also, if only to illustrate that present problems are not new, that when the coming into operation of the Single Act was delayed because the courts in Ireland decided that a referendum was needed, the Belgian Presidency took the view – which was accepted – that the Council should behave as though majority voting was in force although it did not come into force for another six months.

This review of how it all began would not be complete unless I referred to the Cecchini Report which I commissioned early in 1986. Although studies of a general nature had been produced by the European Parliament, notably the Albert-Ball report, there was little firm evidence to support the generally accepted view that great economic advantages would flow from creating a Single European Market. The Cecchini Report was intended to fill that gap and it did so brilliantly and authoritatively. It did more than anything to underpin the intellectual appeal of the White Paper Programme by hard analysis of its economic benefits. It was and remains a mine of information about the flawed operation of the European Market as it then existed and the immense opportunities which would be opened up by its integration.

I now come to the end of that part of the story I was asked to cover. I do not propose trespassing on the ground to be covered by other speakers. But I would like to quote what was said by the Heads of Government at Hannover in June 1988 as I came to the end of my term of office:

> "The European Council considers that this major objective . . . has now reached the point where it is irreversible, a fact accepted by those engaged in economic and social life."

No one could have hoped for a more fitting epitaph.

> "Si monumentum requiris, circumspice."

Finally may I say this. Of necessity this lecture is "One Man's Story". But I fully recognise that the roots of any major reform go very deep, that many people have contributed both to the ideas and the inspiration underlying that reform and many hands have shared the work of implementation. In any great story there will be many unsung heroes. But let me not be thought uncaringly to have paid too little homage to their contribution.